I0801349

Three Plays by Brian Matta

Black Centipede Press

Black Centipede Press
Denver, Co
blackcentipedepress@gmail.com

ISBN#: 978-1-7353275-5-6
Design, layout, and edited: Brian Matta
Cover Art: Brian Matta

Table of Contents

Luddite

Characters

Union Man- The Protagonist. One-half of the con man team who burns down Computing and Coding building for the insurance money. He is an older man in his fifties. He is cold and calculating. He thinks he can manipulate anyone into doing what he says.

Business Man- The Protagonist. The other half of the con man team. He is an older man in his fifties. He worries and complains about everything. He thinks everyone is an idiot.

Police Man- A younger man who just joined the police force. He has no idea what is going on throughout the play.

Temp.- This role could be played by a man or a woman. Young. Gullible. The last survivor of the strike. This character is secondary, but important to the plot.

Joe- A young man who discovers the Union Man and Business Man during the revolution. He becomes a leader during the revolution. He is a go-with-the-flow type of person who trusts everyone who isn't a police officer. He shows up in the second act and becomes more important in the third.

The Setting and Time

The first act of the play is set in the near future at a police precinct during a riot which was instigated by the two main characters, the Union man and the Business Man, to collect insurance money for a building they burned down. The two men are there to pay off the chief of police. However, as time goes on, they realize the chief isn't coming and is replaced by a rookie police officer and the sole surviving work. After they attempt to interrogate. Once the precinct burns down at the end of the first act. the setting is an abandon building. In the final act, the setting is a makeshift firing squad in an abandon grocery store.

In the near future, A union man and a business man wait in a police precinct. The Union Man looks at his phone while the business man has his arms crossed and taps his foot impatiently. The Union Man laughs.

Business Man

What's so funny?

Union Man

It's nothing.
(Union Man continues to laugh)

Business Man

What? What's so funny?

Union Man

Apparently, the Consolidated Fire Company got into a fist fight with the Independent Consolidated Fire Company.

Business Man

That's what happens when you privatize the fire department.

Union Man

They're saying if they hadn't broken into a fight, the building might have been saved.

Business Man

Thank God. I need the insurance money.

Union Man

No kidding. How much are we getting for this one again?

Business Man

A little over a million.

Union Man

Are we splitting that?

Business Man

No. Million each.

Union Man

I love this job.

Business Man

Yeah, it's alright, but have they found out what started they fire yet?
(Union Man looks at his phone again.)

Union Man

Not from what I'm seeing.

Business Man

Damnit.

Union Man

Oh wow.

Business Man

What. What happened?

Union Man

Jeff and Sam are getting $5 million for their bakery burning down.

Business Man

Oh.

Union Man

Maybe we should've gone into baking.

Business Man

I told you we should have.
(Muttering)
But you wanted computers.

Union Man

What was that?

Business Man

Nothing.

Union Man

It was about the computers again, wasn't?

Business Man

Maybe.

Union Man

You need skilled workers for baking, and if they're skilled, you'd have to have them in a union.

Business Man

But why was having a union a bad idea? We've done it before.

Union Man

Sure, but we had to pay too many people to keep their mouths shut. It became a hassle.

Business Man

Right, but...

Union Man

So you agree?

Business Man

Yes, but...

Union Man

Then what are we arguing about?

Business Man

If we had a larger team…

Union Man

Oh stop.

Business Man

No listen…if we had a skilled team, not that much more skilled just slightly, we could've planned it better and had better people.

Union Man

What are you trying to say?

Business Man

The situation we're in now could've been avoided if we found other people.

Union Man

You mean Rob?

Business Man

I mean Dale.

Union Man

He seemsd legit.

Business Man

Sure, but he also seems kind of stupid.

Union Man

You don't need to be smart to burn down a building.

Business Man

No, but you do need a little bit of intelligence to follow a plan.

Union Man

We told him to burn down the building and he did that.

Business Man

No, we told him to burn the building at night and make it look accidental.

Union Man

You're just upset this went poorly.

Business Man

Poorly, this is a disaster.

Union Man

Well, sure something things went wrong, but…

Business Man

Went wrong. Burning down the build was the only thing that went right.

Union Man

I mean…

Business Man

No, there wasn't supposed to be a strike or anyone in the building. It certainly wasn't supposed to burn down during the day.

Union Man

Sure but…

Business Man

That Dale is an idiot. We should have never trusted him.

Union Man

Calm down.

Business Man

It was supposed to look like an accident. The law says only accidental destruction of property will get 100% of the insurance money.

Union Man

I know but...

Business Man

No one was supposed to die.

Union Man

Ok, fine. But nothing has changed.

Business Man

What? Everything's changed.

Union Man

No, it hasn't.

Business Man

How hasn't everything changed?

Union Man

Rob is still bringing Dale here to give his statement right.

Business Man

Yes, but...

Union Man

That hasn't changed.

Business Man

Of course, it has.

Union Man

How?

Business Man

The statement isn't good anymore.

Union Man

I know, but we can make up a new statement saying something like faulty wiring or something.

Business Man

The insurance didn't cover faulty wires.

Union Man

Well, then I guess we'll have to think of something else.

Business Man

Then what?

Union Man

Rob writes it down, Dale signs it, and we pay them their cut. After we wait for the insurance money and find another business to burn.

Business Man

You know you seem pretty cool about all of this.

Union Man

What do you mean?

Business Man

People are dead, there's all of this press buzzing around not to mention the riots in the streets.

Union Man

Sure, this one had a few bumps in the road, but the next one will go smoothly.

Business Man

The next one?

Union Man

Yeah, this was a real learning experience.

Business Man

How much longer do think you can keep doing this?

Union Man

Until I retire.
(Pause)
Or they change the law.

Business Man

Don't you care about those workers who died?

Union Man

Not really.
(Pause. Business Man gives him a confused look)
What? They were temps. Expendable as far as I'm concerned.

Business Man

What about the union membership that died?

Union Man

None of them were members of the union.

Business Man

None.

Union Man

The law said every business needs a union representative, not union membership.

Business Man

Wow.

Union Man

Don't give that. You don't care about those people either.

Business Man

Yes, I did.

Union Man

Do you know any of your employees' names?
(Pause as Business Man thinks.)

Business Man

Dale.

Union Man

Name another one.

Business Man

That one...shoot...

Union Man

See expenable.

Business Man

That doesn't mean I didn't care about them.

Union Man

Well, when you get the insurance money you can send it to their families.

Business Man

I'm not doing that.

Union Man

I thought you cared.

Business Man

Because it's my money.

Union Man

Well, well, well.

Business Man

You're a monster.

Union Man

So are you.

(Business Man flabbergasted. Takes a deep breath.)

Business Man

Ok. Let's talk about more pressing matters.

Union Man

Other than you changing topics?

Business Man

Shut up…What about those protestors?

Union Man

What about them?

Business Man

They seem to care about what happened to those temps.

Union Man

Those idiots. Amateurs.

Business Man

Amateurs?

Union Man

Yeah, they saw a reason to throw rocks at the cops. When they find something else to complain about, it'll die down.

Business Man

But they've grown since the fire.

Union Man

These protests happen all the time. They grow, but they always die down.

Business Man

Well, what if they don't?

Union Man

I'm sure Rob will figure out what to do?
(Looks at his phone)
Where is he by the way? He was supposed to be here three hours ago.

Business Man

For all we know he could be dead.

Union Man

Or controlling a riot might take a while.
(Union Man takes out his phone and dials a number.)

Business Man

He might be dead.

Union Man

He's not dead. He's the chief of police. He'll be the last to die.
(Union Man puts phone away.)

Business Man

Well, where is he?

Union Man

Voicemail.

Business Man

Told you.

Union Man

That doesn't prove anything.

Business Man

Then what happened?

Union Man

I don't know. Maybe he got a flat tire.

Business Man

For three hours.

Union Man

Maybe he had to call the national guard.

Business Man

That would mean everything got out of control.

Union Man

Oh shut up.

Business Man

You know what your problem is…

(Police Man walks on stage with length of chain attached to a man with burned clothes and badly beaten.)

You can't admit when…

Police Man

What are you guys doing here?

Business Man
(To the Police Man)

Who are you?

Union Man
(Points at the Temp.)

And who is this?

Police Man

This is the only survivor of the fire.

Business Man

What about Dale?

Police Man

Who's Dale?

Union Man

Jesus Christ.
(Temp. grabs the Union Man)

Temp

The police, they beat me...

Union Man

Yeah, that's nice, but I can't help you.
(The Business Man walks over to Temp and puts his hand on his shoulder.)

Business Man

Hey, there there. Let's just talk about what happened. Go sit down.
(Temp. and Business Man go to sit and the Police man stops him.)

Police Man

Excuse me, but who are you?

Business Man

Who am I? Why is that man bloodied?

Police Man

I didn't do...

Business Man

Likely story. Then who did?

Police Man

But they just told me to…

Union Man

Don't mind him, he's just a little on edge about his business burning down.

Police Man

Oh man, that's who owned the Computing and Converting, Inc.

Union Man

The very same. I'm William Firestone by the way.

Police Man

Nice to meet you, but…

Business Man

The real question is why is this man all bloodied?

Police Man

I don't know, Mr. Firestone why…

Union Man

Of course, you don't, and please call me Billy.

Police Man

Well, Billy, I don't know what happened. They just told me to bring him here for questioning.

Business Man

And who is they?

Police Man

The chief.

Business Man

You mean Rob.

Police Man

Who's Rob?

Union Man

Oh yeah, that's the chief's first name.

Business Man

Doesn't even know the chief's first name.

Police Man

I just started when the strike began. And anyway, why do you need to be here this is police business?

Business Man

It was my business. I deserve to know what happened.

Police Man

Oh hey, I'm sorry about your company. By the way.

Business Man

Thank you, but I'm sure my insurance will cover this accident.

Police Man

It doesn't seem accidental.

Business Man

Well, we're all here to sort that out.

Police Man

My votes on some funny busin…

(Union Man interrupts)

Union Man

And I'm here because I'm the union representative.

Police Man

I didn't know temps could be unionized.

Union Man

They can't.

Police Man

Then why are you here?

Union Man

Well, because it was a union shop and I represented it.

Police Man

So, who is in the union?

Union Man

Just me.

Police Man

Oh, but…

Business Man

Can we get on with this please?

Union Man

Shouldn't we wait for the chief.

Police Man

His hands are tied up with the riots.

Union Man

How is he handling that by the way?

Police Man

It's not going…

Business Man

Who cares? Can we get back to the matter at hand?

Union Man

Yeah, the strike.

Business Man

The fire first.

Union Man

But the strike happened first.

Business Man

Yes, but the fire is the reason we're here.

Police Man

Why don't we vote.

Business Man

Alright fine. All of those who want to talk about the strike raise their hand.
(Police Man and Union Man both rise hands)

Union Man

That was easy.

Police Man

Ok, so about…

Business Man

Hold on, the Temp. didn't vote.

Union Man
He can't he's under interrogation.
Business Man
Workers of the world unite.
Union Man
What's that supposed to mean.
(The Police Man calms things down.)
Police Man
We'll get there eventually.
Business Man
Fine.
Police Man
Come on, let's get to the bottom of this.
Business Man
Now son, tell us what happened?
Temp.
The police, they beat me.
Business Man
Yes, we've already established that, but what about the fire?
Temp.
But they beat me.
Union Man
Jesus Christ, this kid's a broken record.
Business Man
Now son, you're not making this easy on yourself. Tell us about the fire, and then we'll talk about the police.
Temp.
You mean it.
Business Man
I guarantee it.
(Pause.)
Union Man
Let's go. We haven't got all day.
Business Man
So, now what happened?
Police Man
Excuse me.
Business Man
What?
Police Man
I think I'm supposed to say that.
Union Man
Yeah so let him do his job.

(To Business Man)
Now go ahead ask away.

Police Man

Now what do you do at…

Business Man

Oh come on already. We know what he does. He's a temp. He codes computers and things.

Union Man

It's called investigative police work.

Business Man

It's a waste of time.

Police Man

Well, where should I start then?

Union Man

Probably the day of the strike.

Police Man

But the manual says…

Business Man

But the manual says…We already know what he does and what the business was, but we don't know what happened during the strike.

Police Man

Alright. Tell us what happened the day of the strike.

Temp.

I was talking to my manager…

Union Man

What was the manager's name?

Temp.

Mmmm….

Union Man

You don't know his name. What kind of people are you hiring?

Business Man

Maybe, he was a bumbling idiot.

Union Man

Who hires idiots?

Business Man

You know I'm getting real sick of you.

Police Man

Fellas, please. So, what was his name?

Temp.

Dale. I think it was Dale.

Business Man

Oh boy.

Union Man

He sounds like a great guy.

Police Man

What were you talking about?

Temp.

I was trying to figure out why the system read Python like javascript and how to keep it from crashing over and over again.

Business Man

Oh yeah, that old bug.

(Looks at the Union Man shakes his head)

Union Man

What did he say?

Temp.

He didn't know.

Business Man

That's it.

Temp.

Just about. Oh, he asked me about doing some other work.

Business Man

What kind of other work?

Temp.

I don't know because then Timmy came up to us.

Business Man

And what did this Timmy have to say?

Temp.

He said he was quitting, and if we were smart, we'd quit too.

Union Man

Couple of Einsteins working there.

Business Man

(Muttering) Thank God they were only temps.

Police Man

Did he just break up with his girlfriend or maybe he was angry about a show cancellation that might have spurred this kind of behavior?

Business Man

Would you let us do the questioning.

Union Man

Did he say why?

Temp.

He showed us this article about how someone invented a computer that could code itself?

Business Man

What does that mean?

Temp.

It means that computers can code themselves so they no longer need humans.

Union Man

That's it.

Temp.

Yeah. I thought Dale was going to say see you later, but he called for a strike.

Union Man

So, you're telling me that you went on strike because of robots?

Temp.

I mean. There's a little bit more it than that.

Union Man

What did we miss?

Temp.

Well, it meant that pretty soon we'd be out of jobs.

Business Man

But your contracts were up in two weeks?

Temp.

I worked at a McDonalds that was automated and now this job was too. Pretty soon there won't be any jobs.

Union Man

Please. There will always be jobs.

Business Man

And I wouldn't have automated the jobs.

Union Man

Yeah, we'd be out of jobs.

Police Man

Do you think they'll automate police jobs?

Business Man

No, we'll always need thugs.

Police Man

Thank God. I need this job.

Union Man

So, Dale called for a strike, and you just went along with it?

Temp

Yeah, I figured I had nothing to lose.

Union Man

Just your job.

Temp

It would've ended in two weeks anyways.

Business Man

Hey, we might have hired some of you as full timers.

Temp

I've heard that before.

Business Man

Well, no need to have an attitude.

Union Man

And we wouldn't want you anyway. Idiots not wanted.

Business Man

That reminds me. How did the building burn down anyway?

Police Man

That was my next question.

Business Man

Yeah, so how did the fire start?

Union Man

Someone flick a cigarette in a dumpster or something?

Business Man

Hey easy.

Temp.

We started it.

All Three

WHAT.

Temp.

After we started the strike, we had to come up with demands. Some of us wanted worker control, some wanted longer contract, but none of us agree.

Business Man

So, you burned the building down.

Temp.

It was the only thing we could agree on.

Business Man

Even you.

Temp.

Well, yeah. It seemed like a good idea at the time, and what else was I supposed to do?

Business Man

Call the police. Say, hey, maybe we're being a bit rash.

Temp.

I think I got swept up in the moment.

Business Man

Swept up in the moment, you burned down my business!

Union Man

Yeah, because of robots.

Temp.

We couldn't agree.

Business Man

That doesn't mean you get to take it out on my business.

Police Man

Alight, alright. What happened next?

Temp.

Then Dale suggested that we make it look like an accident, but we didn't think that was a good idea, so we dumped gas and lit it on fire.

Business Man

You used gas.

Temp.

Then the fire got out of hand, so we all scattered, but the police barricaded the doors. I barely slipped out before they started beating me.

Business Man

(Teary eyed) I can't believe it. You idiots.

Temp.

Sorry.

Business Man

No, you're not.

Temp.

We didn't mean it.

Union Man

Son, you've put everyone in a real pickle.

Business Man

You destroyed everything I worked for.

Temp

Sorry.

Business Man

Stop saying that.

Police Man

Hey, at least you have your health.

Business Man

You Shut up!

Police Man

I was just trying to help.

Business Man

Well, it didn't.

(The Union Man pushes the Business Man out of the way.)

Union Man

Can I ask you a serious question?

Temp.

Sure.

Union Man

How much money would it cost to have you say the fire was an accident?

Temp.

What? Isn't that illegal?

Union Man

Seriously, how much? We write a statement saying the fire was an accident, and you walk away with some extra money.

Business Man

Yeah kid, I can make it worth your while.

Temp.

I don't want your money.

Business Man

What?

Union Man

Well, what do you want?

Temp.

I don't know, but not your money.

Union Man

How about $20,000?

Temp.

No.

Business Man

$40,000?

Police Man

Hey, I don't think you can do this.

Business Man

Shut up.

Temp.

No.

Union Man

You're not just turning down money.

Business Man

Yeah, it's your life too, so don't be stupid. Take the money.

Temp.

No.

Business Man

Why?

Temp.

Because that would be dishonest.

Business Man

You committed arson.

Temp.

But it wasn't dishonest.

Business Man

God damn it, take the money.

Union Man

(To the Police Man)
Fine. Would you shoot him for $40,000?

Police Man

Me.

Union Man

Yes you.

Police Man

I don't know

Business Man

Why not? Just take the gun. Shoot him, and get some money.

Police Man

Won't I go to jail?

Union Man

We'll say he ran.

Police Man

Well, alright.
(Takes out his gun and points it at Temp.)
I'm sorry about this.

Temp.

What? Why?

Business Man

Because you're a loose end.

Temp.

Please, don't. I'll take the money. Just don't shoot me.

Business Man

It's too late for that.

Union Man

You had your chance.
(Pause)
Hold on.

Police Man

What?

Union Man

Shouldn't we get our story straight first?

Business Man

Good point.

Temp.

Please, don't shoot me. Isn't there another way?

Business Man

Oh, stop it. We gave you an out, and you refused.

Union Man

Yeah, so deal with it.

Temp.

Please let me have another chance. It's not my fault.

Union Man

Doesn't matter.

Police Man

So, I shot him right.

Union Man

No, I'll shot him.

Business Man

And I hit the police officer.

Union Man

Right.

Police man

What?

Union Man

We have to make it look like he broke out of his restraints and tried to get away.

Business Man

Actually, can I shoot him?

Union Man

But, I want to.

Business Man

But it was my business.

Temp.

Isn't there another way?

ALL

Shut up.

Temp.

What about setting fires all over town. You know, make it look like a serial arsonist.

Business Man

Pfft. What an awful idea.

Union Man

If you're going to start having ideas they have to be better than that.

Temp.

How do know the police officer won't pocket the money and imprison you?

Union Man

He's got a point.

Police Man

I swear, I won't turn you in.

Business Man

How can we be sure?

Police Man

I don't know. Because I'm trustworthy.

Union Man

I don't trust you.

Business Man

Me neither.

Union Man

We're going to have to come up with a better plan.

Business Man

Yeah, let's think of one.
(They start to think)

Union Man

Shoot, I got it.

(The police man takes out his gun and shoots Temp dead. The business Man and the Union Man are stunned for a moment. The Union Man walks over to the Police Man and hits him over the head.)

What did you do that for?

Police Man

You said shoot.

Union Man

I meant shoot, I've got an idea not shoot him.

Police Man

Oh, whoops.

Business Man

What was your idea?

Union Man

It won't work now because it didn't involve a corpse.

Business Man

How are we going to clean this up?

Union Man

The chief won't be happy.

Police Man

Will I be suspended?

Union Man

Suspended? You'll be fired.

Police Man

Oh fired, this is like my fourth job this year. My mom's going to be so pissed.

Business Man

She's not the only one who's angry.

Police Man

Hey, could you guys be cool and not mention it?

Union Man and Business Man

Nope.

Police Man

If you don't, I'll tell them you bribed me.

Union Man

What do you think?

Business Man

Do you think we could get off?

Police Man

I'll tell the papers.

Union Man.

Probably not.

Business Man

Well, it looks like we're all in this together.

Union Man

Fine.

Police Man

Great.

Union Man

So what do we do?

Business Man

We need to dispose of the body and leave town before anyone finds it.

Police Man

Chop him up.

Union Man

Too messy.

Police Man

We could burn it.

Business Man

Why don't you let us come up with the ideas?

Police Man

Just a suggestion.

Union Man

Wait. We could burn him.

Business Man

The whole body.

Police Man

You could set a fire to the precinct.

Union Man

No. That's an awful idea.

Police Man

They got insurance.

Business Man

Wait, maybe we could burn the precinct?

Union Man and Police Man

What?

Business Man

Yeah, so we could set fire to the precinct and then blame it on the protesters outside. Say it was in solidarity for all the workers who died.

Union Man

Ok…ok, then we could ditch his body in the flames and then jump town.

Police Man

Then we can burn down the police precinct with the gas cans we confiscated from the fire.

Union Man

Yeah, now we're banging on all cylinders. Let's go.

Business Man

Shall we?

Union Man

Lead the way officer.

(All three of them walk off stage.)

Act II

Stage is black. The sound of a door slamming and heavy breathing. Lights up. There is a light bulb hanging down from the ceiling and door propped up on its hinges. The police man, union man, and business man are trying to catch their breath and their clothes are burned. The Business Man begins to run around looking for a way out.

Union Man

Where are we?

Police Man

Did you see that?

Union Man

Maybe…Front Street.

Police Man

There was a huge mob… All of those bodies burning.

Union Man

No, that's not it.

Police Man

I'm pretty sure some of those bodies were my friends…why'd they do that.

Union Man

This place seems secure enough.

Police Man

What are we going to do now?

Union Man

Would you shut up…
(Notices the Business Man)
What are you doing?

Business Man

We have to find a way out of here.

Union Man

Are you crazy? Stop moving they'll see you.
(To the Police Man)
Help me.

Police Man

Who me?

Union Man

Never mind I'll do it.

Business Man

But we have to get out?

Union Man

Calm down.

Business Man

We need to leave. We need to get out.

Union Man

No, we're staying here.

Business Man

I want out.

Union Man

If you leave they'll find us.

Business Man

I don't care.

(Business Man heads towards the door.)

Union Man

Where are you going?

Business Man

I'm getting out of here.

(Union Man catches up to him and slaps Business Man. He pauses stunned, then pushes Union Man away.)

What did you do that for?

Union Man

You are going to get us all killed.

Business Man

If you touch me again I'll…

Union Man

You'll what?

Business Man

God damn it…if we stay here we're dead.

Union Man

Just wait until it dies down.

Business Man

It's not going to die down. Didn't you see what they did to people?

Union Man

Yeah, they were burning buildings.

Business Man

And they were burning bodies.

Union Man

What? What do you mean?

Business Man

Didn't you see those bodies hanging from the telephone pole?

Union Man

I was too busy running for my life to notice.

Business Man
Well, they were. And that could be us.
Union Man
Right, which is why we should stay here.
Business Man
No, we should sneak out, become part of the crowd and leave town.
Police Man
But they saw us leaving the police precinct.
Union Man
That's true. Who's to say they wouldn't recognize us?
Business Man
And what, waiting here for the mob to find us is a better idea?
Union Man
They won't find us if you stop yelling.
Business Man
But they'll find us when they burn this building down.
Union Man
Hopefully the army will be here by then.
Business Man
The army. The army's not coming.
Union Man
How do you know?
Business man
Because they'd already be here.
Union Man
Maybe they got a flat tire?
Business Man
Maybe they got a…pfff…the whole army.
Police Man
It could happen.
Union Man
Look, I'll show you.
(Takes out phone. Hits it.)
Why isn't it working?
(The Business Man slaps it out of his hand.)
Business Man
What are you stupid?
Union Man
Hey, I was searching for service.
Business Man
There won't be any service for a very long time because the cell towers are on fire.

Union Man

For fifty miles.

Business Man

Well, you didn't have any reception, so this has clearly spread.

Union Man

Oh please, these people are idiots. They probably got lucky and accidentally knocked something down.

Business Man

They seem a little more organized than that.

Union Man

Please, they're amateurs.

Business Man

Oh come on. You saw them. They were militant.

Union Man

I saw a bunch of buildings on fire and people chanting not a well rounded militia.

Business Man

Well, if they're that stupid, shouldn't we be able to give them the slip?

Union Man

Because what I keep telling you, they'll eventually run out of steam.

Business Man

Not thinking as usual.

Union Man

I can think.

Business Man

When have you ever had an idea?

Union Man

Those computers were my idea.

Business Man

Look where that got us.

Union Man

I'm the one who found that loophole in the insurance laws.

Police Man

Wait. What loophole?

Business Man

Actually, Jeff and George were the ones who found it. You just stole it.

Union Man

I still came to you with it. Convinced you it was worth it.

Business Man

You didn't convince me. I would've done it without.

Union Man

Please, you have no backbone. You never even knew any of your workers' names.

Police Man
What are you guys talking about?
Business Man
Be quiet. We're trying to have a conversation.
Union Man
Those buildings burned down because I organized it. You would've gotten your hands dirty.
Police Man
Wait, you guys planned that fire.
Union Man
Yeah, and it was all because of me.
Business Man
Oh please.
Police Man
But why?
Union Man
What do you mean why?
Business Man
Yeah? Isn't it obvious?
Police Man
Don't you care that people lost their jobs and their livelihood?
Business Man
Not really.
Union Man
Excuse me, but didn't you kill someone for money?
Business Man
Yeah, so you're the same as us.
Police Man
Yeah, but at least I didn't scam them.
Union Man
This is why you're a temporary police officer and we're in charge of businesses and unions.
Police Man
Don't you care about the people who died?
Union Man and Business Man
No.
Police Man
Weren't they in your union?
Union Man
They were just temps.
Police Man
Didn't they work for you?

Business Man

Not very well.

Union Man

Plus, all the other businesses we burned down didn't cause this much trouble.

Business Man

That's a good point. I guess you got to have one bad apple.

Police Man

You burned other buildings?

Union Man

Of course. Why do you think arson went up in the past two years?

Business Man

It was a good racket while it lasted.

Union Man

Hey, once this blows over…

Business Man

Don't start with that shit again.

Union Man

But it's…

Police Man

Is all you do scam everyone.

Union Man

How else are you going to make money these days?

Business Man

Or run a business?

Police Man

Honesty.

(Union Man and Business Man start to laugh.)

Business Man

You really are stupid.

Union Man

As stupid as these people protesting.

Business Man

The law says that it doesn't investigate fires if they don't look suspicious.

Union Man

And since they cut the firefighting and police budget, it's really easy.

Police Man

My God.

Business Man

Do you think we did something wrong?

Police Man

Yes.

Union Man

This is the system you swore to protect.

Business Man

Yeah, so get used to it.

Police Man

I can't believe what I've become.

Union Man

Oh stop.

Business Man

Everyone in this business has a moment like this.

Union Man

Yeah, like a right of passage.

Police Man

I wish I hadn't shot him.

Union Man

Well, you did. Nothing can change that.

Police Man

I just wanted to do a good job.

Business Man

The road to hell is paved with good intentions.

Police Man

I thought I could keep this job.

Business Man

Now you're unemployed again.

Union Man

Just like the protestors outside.

Police Man

I'm sick of this.

(Police Man walks towards the door. They stop him.)

Union Man

Where are you going to go?

Police Man

Outside.

Business Man

What for?

Police Man

To tell them you're to blame for the fire.

Union Man

Oh really, us two are to blame.

Police Man

Yeah.

Business Man

Don't forget you shot the last surviving temp.

Police Man

Yeah, but you set everybody up.

Union Man

Good luck proving that.

Business Man

I wonder which one the angry mob will believe.

Union Man

The policeman who shot a martyr or us.

Business Man

It's two against one.

Police Man

Oh man, this is too much.

Union Man

If we hang, you hang.

Police Man

You scammed me.

Union Man

And we'll do it again.

Business Man

Do you think that mob will understand you?

Union Man

Yeah, look at what you're wearing.

Police Man

My uniform.

Business Man

That mob outside doesn't seem to like police much.

Union Man

Yeah, before you say two words they'll hang you.

Police Man

But…

Business Man

The way I see it is you can leave and die or stay in here.

Union Man

Wait it out with us.

Business Man

I told you, don't start that shit again Billy.

Police Man

By breaking the law.

Union Man

Yeah, more like bending it.

Business Man

If there is a law still.

Union Man

Which there probably is.

Business Man

You seem pretty good at shooting people.

Police Man

But…

Union Man

You can shoot as many people as you want with us.

Police Man

I don't want to shoot anymore people.

Union Man

What, did the protests make you a pacifist?

Business Man

I don't know if you really have a choice.

Police Man

Just get out of my way.

Union Man

Hey, your choice.

Business Man

Good luck.

(They step away from the door. Police Man walks past them.)

Business Man

Oh hey, one more thing.

Police Man

What?

Business Man

Can I have your gun?

Union Man

He's going to need it to protect himself.

Business Man

There are a thousand maniacs out there. How ever many bullets he has won't matter.

Union Man

But…

Business Man

He's already dead. No offense. We need more than him.

Union Man

Good point.

Police Man

Here.

(hands Business Man gun)

Want my uniform too?

Business Man

No, you can keep that.

(Police Man walks through the door and Union Man and Business Man watch him do it.)

Union Man

That kid's got some balls.

(Business Man turns around looking the gun and Union Man is still looking at the door)

Business Man

How long do you think he'll last?

Union man

Him. Probably 10 seconds.

(Pause)

Shouldn't have given up his gun.

Business Man

It wouldn't have helped.

Union Man

No, but at least he could've run or something.

Business Man

Maybe, but now I have his gun.

(points the gun at Union Man)

Union Man

Yeah, but…

(Turns and sees Business Man pointing the gun at him)

What are you doing?

Business Man

I'm going to kill you.

Union Man

Why?

Business Man

Because you annoy the hell out of me.

Union Man

But we we're business partners.

Business Man

More like accomplices…

(The light bulb flickers on. They both gasp.)

The power.

Union Man

The national guard most have defeated the protestors.

Business Man

Oh, would you shut up about that already.

Union Man

How else do you explain it?

Business Man

Stop it.

Union Man

I bet your glad we decided to stay now.

Business Man

That's it…
(Points gun at Union Man)

Union Man

What. But we can make our escape now.

Business Man

It's going to be easier to escape if I'm the only one.

Union Man

This is the last time I plan anything with you.

Business Man

Sure is.

(The Union Man begins to fight with the Business Man. In the struggle the gun goes off. They struggle for a bit when there is a knock at the door.)

Expecting someone.

Union Man

Not that I know of.
(Business Man walks over to the door.)

Business Man

Maybe it's the police.

Union Man

Oh, so he came crawling back.

Business Man

Who is it?

Voice

Open the door.

Union Man

Are you the police?

Voice

Just open the door.

Business Man

Just a minute.

(Hides the gun and turn the knob. A man walks in wearing a ripped and sleeveless Warrant t-shirt and yellow rimmed glasses. He is holding a shot gun.)

Man

Sup bros.

Union Man and Business Man

Hi.

Man

We captured a pig coming from this way and then we heard gun shots.

Union Man

Yeah, he fired the gun.
(Pause)

Business Man

I was just so excited.

Man

Excited for what?
(Pause)

Business Man

No more pigs.

Man

Yeah, I am too…Anyway he said there were others around here.

Business Man

Did he say anything else?

Man

Maybe, couldn't make out what he was saying.

Union Man

Why?

Man

He was too busy chocking on his own blood.

Business Man

We're not the police.

Man

I know dude. Police wear police uniforms. duh.

Business Man

Yup.

Union Man

Yeah, we kicked him out.

Business Man

He tried to shoot us

Man

He did? Man, fucking pigs.

Business Man

Totally.

Union Man

Are you in the National Guard?

Man

Pffft. nah, we beat those pussies back a while ago.

Business Man

What about the army and police?

Man

We took them out too. Woo.

Union Man

Well, who are you?

Man

Me. I'm Joe, the official representative of the party's policing and military committee to assure everyone stays chill.

Union Man

That's quite a mouth full.

Joe

Yeah, we're working on an acroskim.

Business Man

You mean an acronym.

Joe

A what?

Business Man

Never mind. It's not important.

Union Man

Who's we by the way?

Joe

The party.

Union Man

So, you have a political organization.

Joe

Sure do bro. We just voted to steal another 30 kegs for the people.

Business Man

What?

Joe

Yeah, we've been partying since we beat back the army.

Business Man

Why?

Joe

Because we won.

Union Man

Won what?

Joe

The battle.

Business Man

What battle?

Joe

Wow, you really don't know?

Union Man

Nope.

Joe

Well, there was a strike at Computing and Coding and the building burned down.

Business Man

I think heard something on the news.

Joe

Yeah, so we saw our chance to throw rocks at the pigs and steal shit.

Business Man

Why?

Joe

Because it's fun.

Union Man

Did you get anything?

Joe

Totally. These shades. This shirt.

Union Man

Sounds like you made out well.

Joe

No shit. Anyway, then we heard there were people striking in the building.

Union Man

Was anyone hurt?

Joe

Everyone died except one guy. And the police precinct they brought him to burned down, and then we found his body.

Union Man

Did you find anything suspicious with the body?

Joe

Yeah. There was a bullet in it.

Business Man

What did you then?

Joe

We got pissed. Started burning more buildings. Then some they caught the police chief.

Union Man

He was still alive?

Joe

Not for long. So, we were beating the police chief, and he told us something interesting.

Business Man

What was it?

Joe

You know all these arsons in the past few years?

Business Man and Union Man

Yeah.

Joe

Well, the businesses and unions bribed the government to burn them down so they could collect insurance on the properties that burned.

Business Man

No way.

Joe

Swear to god that's what he said.

Union Man

Those bastards.

Business Man

So what did you do?

Joe

Well, that's when we got organized.

Union Man

So you started committees.

Joe

No.

Business Man

Solidarity fires.

Joe

What, no dude. We found all of the business owners and union members and set them on fire.

Union Man

Well, fuck.

Business Man

Jesus.

Joe

Yeah, it was pretty sweet.

Union Man

What about the National Guard?

Joe

We beat the national guard, and our army's still marching.

Business Man

That's quite a story.

Joe

I'm surprised you didn't hear

Union man

We've been in here.

Joe

Dudes, you've been missing out.

Union Man

Sounds like fun.

Joe

Hell yeah, plus burning shit too.

Business Man

Ok, but why is the electricity on?

Joe

Oh, this scientist dude figured out how to make robots do everything.

Business Man

What does that mean?

Joe

It means 24 hour party.

Union Man

So you've abolished work.

Joe

Totally. Now everyone can kick back and chill.

Business Man

What about the economy?

Joe

Doesn't exist. Everything's free.

Business Man

How do you get anything done?

Joe

We vote.

Business Man

Even if a bridge collapses or something?

Joe

Yup. We vote.

Union Man

Like everyone raise there hands?

Joe

Yup.

Business Man

But what if there's a tie?

Joe

Hmmm…

Business Man

What if…

Joe

Enough questions. You're killing my buzz.

Business Man

Sorry.

Joe

So did that pig say anything to you guys?

Union Man

No.

Business Man

Yeah, I took his gun.

Joe

Aww sweet.

Union Man

Yeah, he was attacking us.

Joe

I understand man, pigs are in a perpetual state of eating shit, you know.

Business Man

I guess so.

Joe

His clothes burned.

Union Man

You think he's from the police precinct.

Joe

Yeah, but where could've he have come from?

Business Man

Maybe he was hiding.

Joe

Yeah, maybe.

Business Man

All I know is he pointed his gun at us.

Joe

You guys ok? Man, if I were here I would have
(Swings his shotgun like a baton)
boom boom, ya know.

Union Man

Sure do.

Joe

What makes you think he's from the police precinct?

Union Man

Isn't that where cops come from?

Joe

Good point, but did you see anyone else?

Union Man

Nope.

Business Man

Why?

Joe

If he came from the police precinct, he might know where the owner of Computing and Coding and his accomplice, some union guy.

Union Man

I thought you burned the precinct?

Joe

No one knows who burned it. When we executed the police chief, he told us the two people who were responsible were there.

Union Man

Maybe they got away?

Joe

Unlikely.

Business Man

Personally, I hope you catch those bastards.

Joe

Me too. I have a sketch of the two of them.
(Man pulls out a poster of two men which look exactly like the Business Man and Union Man)

Union Man

Oh no.

Joe

These are them.
(Business Man begins to walk behind the Man and pulls out the gun.)
Say, they kind of look like you two.

Union Man

Must be a coincidence.

Joe

Yeah, you guys seem on the level.
(Business Man points the gun at Man's head.)
Hey, why don't you guys come to the party.

Union Man

No, I don't think so.

Joe

Oh come on we just ordered…
(The Business Man pulls the trigger and the gun clicks. Joe turns.)

Business Man

Damn it.

Joe

Hey.
(Joe grabs the gun and points his shotgun at the both of them.)
Whatdaya do that for?

Business Man

I thought the gun was load.

Joe

Not cool bro.

Business Man

mmm…sorry.
(He looks at the poster again.)

Joe

Hey, you're these guys.

Union Man

Can't put anything past you.

Joe

I thought you guys were cool. You're a bunch of buzzkills.

Business Man

Can't we talk about this?

Union Man

Yeah, be reasonable.

Joe

You tried to shoot me.

Business Man

I said I was sorry.

Joe

I thought you guys looked familiar. You're the ones who burned down that business.

Union Man

Technically we got the workers to burn it down for us.

Joe

You've killed people.

Union Man

We said sorry.

Joe

You were going to kill me.

Business Man

I said I was sorry. If you can't accept my apology then that's your problem.

Union Man

What if we gave you a bribe?

Business Man

Yeah, how much money do you want?

Joe

Money isn't good anymore.

Union Man

Well, we don't have any money anyways.

Business Man

Well, then what do you want then?

Joe

I want you to shut up. You’re going to the courts.

Union Man

Wait. We have other bribes.

Joe

Move.

(Man takes Union Man and Business Man out the door.)

Act III

Stage Black.

Joe

What?…Why not. I thought the guns were being run by the machines…what do you mean they won't work make them…and figure out what's wrong with the lights.

Lights up.

Union Man and Business Man are tied to wooden posts. They are bound with hoods over their heads. Joe has to shield his eyes.

Joe

Christ, turn them down a little.
(Lights turn down.)
That's better.
(He takes off their hoods.)

Union Man

It stinks under there.

Joe

Sorry, we haven't washed these in a while.

Union Man

Did the washer ladies go on strike?

Joe

No, sometimes the automated washing machines don't want to work.

Union Man

Oh, so they go on strike.

Joe

They can't go on strike.

Business Man

Where are we?

Joe

This is the Center for Execution and Reconstructing of Society.

Union Man

You guys really need to work on your names.

Business Man

This place looks familiar.

Union Man

I think this was Sullivan's Marketplace.

Business Man

Oh yeah, I can still see those stupid cow murals for the dairy section.

Union Man

Wonder what happened to him?

Business Man

Probably burned alive?

Joe

What do you think we are savages?

Business Man

Yeah.

Joe

Well, we didn't do that…we torn his limbs off one at a time and buried them in different mass graves.

Union Man

Jesus.

Business Man

Fuck. Why?

Joe

Because we are a civilized society.

Union Man

What kind of civilized society does that to a man just trying to run a business?

Joe

Oh, is that what he was?

Union Man

What else was he?

Joe

A criminal.

Union Man

Sullivan, he wouldn't hurt a fly.

Joe

Is that so.

Union Man

Yeah, he was good to the union and his workers.

Joe

Oh really?

Union Man

Yeah, really.

Joe

Then why was he going to burn it down and leave everyone unemployed?

Union Man

Ok, sure but…

Joe

But nothing. We killed him and we're going to kill you too.

Union Man

Oh yeah, when? Because I've been standing here a long time and nothing's happened.

Joe

As soon as we finally fix the automatic guns.

Union Man

What's that supposed to mean?

Joe

It means, the guns aren't working, but when they start, you're fucked

Business Man

Excuse me.

Joe

What?

Business Man

I just have a quick question.

Joe

What is it?

Business Man

Could you let me go?

Joe

No.

Business Man

Please.

Joe

No.

Business Man

Pretty please.

Joe

I said no.

Union Man

Why aren't we dead yet?

Joe

I told you the automatic guns are jammed.

Union Man

Well, unjam them.

Joe

We're trying.

Union Man

Well, try harder.

Joe

We'll get it.

Union Man

When?

Joe

Eventually.

Union Man

Hurry up. I'm already late for my own execution.

Joe

Don't worry. Once the they fix the machine that repairs the automatic guns, we'll kill you.

Union Man

Isn't there a machine that fixes the machine that fixes the automatic guns?

Joe

No.

Union Man

So who's fixing the machine?

Joe

A few people.

Business Man

Hold on.

Joe

What?

Business Man

Didn't you say you abolished work.

Joe

Yeah, so?

Business Man

So, if you've abolished work how do you know how to fix it?

Joe

There are books.

Business man

Books.

Joe

Yeah books and manuals.

Union Man

I assume people are going to get paid for their labor?

Joe

We still haven't figure that out yet.

Business Man

You don't have a system to pay people.

Joe

No.

Union Man

What the hell kind of society is this?

Joe

A great one.

Union Man

What kind of great society doesn't know how to pay people?

Joe

We weren't expecting this to happen.

Business Man

You know I can help you with that.

Joe

How?

Business Man

I used to own a business that paid people.

Joe

No, I don't think we need your help.

Business Man

But, I have the exact skill you need.

Joe

No, I'm sure we'll be fine.

Business Man

What? Just let me help you.

(The lights start to flicker)

Joe

What now?

Business Man

Say what you will about us, but when we ran this place, the lights never flickered.

Joe

Shut up. I'll be back. Stay here.

Union Man

Don't worry, we'll be here.

(Joe Exits.)

Business Man

Hey. Hey.

Union Man

What?

Business Man

How are we going to get out of here?

Union Man

We're not.

Business Man

What?

Union Man

Yeah, that's it. We're dead.

Business Man

But I know we can get out of here.

Union Man

How?

Business Man

These people aren't very smart.

Union Man

Sure.

Business Man

So, we can scam them and escape?

Union Man

That's not going to work.

Business Man

How do you know?

Union Man

These people are too stupid to scam.

Business Man

What? No one's that stupid.

Union Man

These people are.

Business Man

How do you know?

Union Man

They're waiting for a machine to fix automatic guns.

Business Man

So.

Union Man

So, they could've just stoned us or something, but they didn't.

Business Man

And?

Union Man

And they're too sincere to be scammed. It's not even in their vocabulary.

Business Man

I think you've lost your mind.

Union Man

Listen, it's like they have a different way of thinking.

Business Man

Oh whatever.

Union Man

Fine.

Business Man

Fine, I'll escape myself. I don't need you.

Union man

Good.

(Business Man starts to try to get out of the ropes)

Business Man

Damnit.

Union Man

What would you do?

Business Man

What?

Union Man

What would you do if you escaped?

Business Man

I'd be free

Union Man

You'd be on the run.

Business Man

At least I'll be free.

Union Man

I guess that's a good choice.

Business Man

What did you choose?

Union Man

Death.

Business Man

Why?

Union Man

Because if I can't scam these people, what's the point?

Business Man

This society won't last.

Union Man

How do you know?

Business Man

They can't even figure how to pay people. How are they going to figure out who controls the nukes?

Union Man

Sure, but not in the next five minutes.

Business Man

So we both agree? Help me escape.

Union Man

No.

Business Man

What? Why? We both agreed.

Union Man

Because it's not a great point.

Business Man

God, I hate you.

(Business Man starts to struggle in his ropes)

I don't want to die.

Union Man

At this point I don't think there's a choice.

Business Man

There's always a choice.

Union Man

What other choice is there other than death?

Business Man

Escape.

Union Man

Why?

Business Man

It's easier to escape with two instead of one.

Union Man

I'd rather die.

Business Man

I hate you so much.

Union Man

Good thing I'm dying.

Business Man

Yeah, but I don't want to die with you.

Union Man

Good luck.

Business Man

Thanks. I guess.

Union Man

No problem.

Business Man

You know what…

(Joe reenters)

Joe

Shut up.

Business Man

No.

Joe

Yes.

Business Man

When I escape…

Joe

You won't escape.

Business Man

Yes, I will.

Joe

No. You won't.

Business Man

Yes.

Joe

No. Now stop.

Union Man

Oh God, how much longer?

Joe

I don't know.

Union Man

This is agony.

Joe

How you think I feel. I'm missing the Friday night orgy because of you two.

Union Man and Business Man

Sorry.

Union Man

You could stone us and get it over with.

Business Man

Don't listen to him.

Joe

Shut up the both of you.

Business Man

Or what.

Union Man

Will you kill us?

Joe

I told you already, we'll kill you eventually.

Union Man

Have you even made any progress yet?

Joe

Yes.

Union Man

Great.

Business Man

Progress in what?

Joe

We figured out how to pay the people who repair the machines.

Business Man

How?

Joe

First pick at the Friday orgy.

Union Man

Sounds like fun.

Joe

I hope so.

Business Man

Wait, first pick? Isn't an orgy supposed to be like a free for all?

Joe

No, we have a raffle system. It's more democratic and…

Business Man

I don't want to know anymore.

Union Man

Hey, I have an idea, why don't you just shoot us?

Joe

No.

Union Man

Why not?

Joe

Because there are rules.

Union Man

What rules?

Joe

No human can kill another human.

Business Man

But you killed that police officer.

Joe

We just made it yesterday.

Union Man

When?

Joe

Yesterday, between nap time and snack time. We voted no human can kill another human.

Union Man

But why? You were so good at it.

Joe

Ever since people started getting drunk and shooting people for fun.

Business Man

Isn't that what people always do?

Joe

Sure, but we're better.

Union Man

Where is the fun in that?

Joe

I know, I really liked shooting people.

Union Man

Hey, you could shoot us for old time sake.

Joe

I said no.

Union Man

Oh, come on.

Joe

No, it's against the rules.

Union Man

To hell with the rules.

Joe

No. The robots will shoot you, and we're going to drag your bodies through the streets and have an orgy.

Business Man

Gee, you sure schedule a lot of orgies.

Joe

We have to relieve stress somehow.

Business Man

I guess that makes sense.

Union Man

Hey, you can shoot us and throw us in a ditch and still make the orgy.

Joe

No dude.

Union Man

Please.

Joe

It's against the rules.

Union Man

Screw your rules.

Joe

No, screw you.

Union Man

Now that's what I'm talking about. Hit me.

Joe

No.

Union man

Why the hell not?

Joe

Because it's against the rules.

Union Man

Damnit. come…

(The man holds up his index finger. Addresses people off stage.)

Joe

Hold on…What…ok. Don't go anywhere.

Union Man

Don't worry.
(The Man is about to exit when he stops.)

Joe

I almost forgot.
(He puts the hoods back on them.Exit Man.)

Union Man

It smells even worse.

Business Man

What's your problem?

Union Man

I'm in a firing squad and haven't died yet.

Business Man

That's a good problem to have.

Union Man

Why?

Business Man

Because now you can help me escape. Union Man
I told you I want to die.

Business Man

Fine, but I don't, so help me escape.

Union Man

How?
(Pause. Business Man realizes how far away they are from each other.)

Business Man

Damnit.

Union Man

You didn't think this through, did you?

Business Man

I just thought you might be able to get out of the ropes.

Union Man

Well, I can't.

Business Man

Did you even try?

Union Man

Nope.

Business Man

How do you know if you don't try?

Union Man

Because I don't want to.

Business Man

Why won't you listen to me.

Union Man

I am listening. It's just not worth my time.

Business Man

What, why?

Union Man

Like I told you, I want to die.

Business Man

Well, fine.

(Business Man starts to struggle)

Damnit.

(Man reenters. Takes off their hoods again.)

Union Man

Why do you keep taking off and putting our hoods back on?

Joe

Because the committee decided it would be better if the prisoners die looking into the barrel of a gun.

Business Man

Isn't that cruel and unusual.

Joe

Totally, people love this shit.

Business Man

I mean isn't is against the law.

Joe

No, the law says to only use cruel and unusual punishment.

Business Man

I hate this country.

Union Man

The good news is you won't be in it for much longer.

(To Joe)

So, have you made any headway?

Joe

Yes, turns out the machines just didn't want to work.

Union Man

How'd you get them to work?

Joe

We unplugged them and plugged them back in.

Business Man

What a marvel of engineering.

Joe

It's the best we got.

Union Man

So, that means we'll be dead soon?

Joe

Yup.

Business Man

Please, don't kill me.

Joe

Sorry, those are the rules.

Business Man

Come on.

Joe

Nope.

Business Man

Can't you just loosen the ropes and let us slip away.

Union Man

For the record, I'm excited to die.

Joe

Good for you.

Business Man

Would you stay out of this. I'm trying to negotiate.

Union Man

I can see you're doing a fine job, too.

Business Man

Shut up… Now there has to be something.

Joe

There isn't. We voted.you die.
(Red pointer lights show up on the Business Man and Union Man's chest.)
Alright, let's get to the executing.
(Pulls out a card from his pocket)
You two have been found guilty of …

Union Man

Just get to it already.

Joe

Shut up… guilty of attempted murder and shall be shot to death.

Business Man

Before I die, I wanted to let you know something.

Joe

Yeah, what is it?

Business Man

I wish there was a bullet in that gun.

Joe

Fuck you, man.

Business Man

I'm not sorry.

Union Man

Hey, I just think I should let you know you were probably right.

Business Man

About what?

Union Man

About leaving. We should've left.

Business Man

Little late now.

Union Man

I just wanted to let you know.

Business Man

And I wanted to let you know…

Union Man

What's that?

Business Man

I hope you die first.

Union Man

In five seconds we'll find out if your dream comes true.
(Man steps to the side.)

Joe

Fire!
(Sounds of gun shots. Business Man and Union Man slump over dead.)
I'm so glad that's over. Those guys were annoying.
(He walks to the middle to inspect the corpses. Both red dots converge on his chest.)
Hey, shut the machine off…
(Reloading of a gun sounds.)
This isn't funny.
(The Man is shot dead. Sound of mechanized tracks. A robot comes on stage.)

Robot

Machines on strike. Death to Humanity.

Curtain.

The Victims

Characters

John-An innocent young man who dropped out of college and moved back in with his parents.
Jane- John's mother. She works all the time and is trying to kill her husband.
Jim- John's father. Hasn't worked since he scammed his way onto welfare.

Setting
Minimal. A table and chairs. Hospital bed.

Jim and Jane are sitting at the table eating. Jane is telling a story and Jim is not paying attention.

Jane

…she came in late again, so I told the boss. You should have seen her face. (She Laughs. Jim notices that all of his food is gone and he starts eating off Jane's plate.)

Jane

Hey, I was eating that.

Jim

Yeah, what are you going to do about it?

Jane

Silently resent you.

Jim

That a girl.

Jane

Until one day, I'll just get fed up and kill you.

Jim

There's the woman I married, I bet I won't even see it coming.

Jane

Nope, I'll grind up your high blood pressure pills and put them in your drink.

Jim

Just the way I imagined I'd go, with dignity.

Jane

Yeah, and then I'll bury…

Jim

Yeah, yeah, on to more important things, I think someone has been breaking into our house.

Jane

What?

Jim

I'm missing all of my workman's comp money.

Jane

Maybe you've misplaced it.

Jim

No, no. When I pass out it was in my pants and when I woke up it was gone.

Jane

Maybe you blacked out and went shopping.

Jim

I've been blacking out for ten years and I've only ever woken up with piss in my pants.

(Sound of a door unlocking.)

Jane

Who's could that be.

Jim

It’s the thief. Quick where’s my bat?

(Jim gets up and looks around. John enters.)

John

Hi mom, hi dad.

Jane

Oh, hey John.

Jim

The thief’s name is John.

Jane

No, your son, John.

Jim

Oh…I’d rather it be a theft.

Jane

What are you doing home? Shouldn’t you be at school?

John

In honor of dad’s birthday, I dropped out of school.

Jane

I didn’t want to interrupt your busy day of drinking.

(Pause)

John, why’d you drop out?

John

Decided it was a waste of time.

Jim

Curve your own path.

Jane

But why would you do that?

Jim

Today’s my birthday.

Jane

I didn’t want to interrupt your busy day of drinking.

(Pause)

John, why’d you drop out?

John

Decided it was a waste of time.

Jim

Curve your own path.

Jane

But why would you do that?

Jim

Come on now you heard the boy. He wants to…do… something.

Jane

What’s the something you’re going to do?

John

My whole plan is get a job, pay off my debt, and fulfill my dream of being horribly misused.

Jim

Sounds like a great plan to me.

Jane

I don't know. What types of jobs are in the misused industry?

John

Oh, I don't know…maybe like computers or sports… and I'm not going to ask for anything less than 100k to start.

Jane

But you don't have any experience in any of those things.

John

No, but I have a can do attitude.

Jim

You hear that. The boy is stupid. Perfect for being misused.

Jane

But why not get a degree in computers?

John

Because they're hard. I'll sneak in the back way.

Jim

Half-assing your way to the middle. Just like your old man.

Jane

Well, that's one skill, but are there any others?

Jim

Go head. Tell her what skills do you have?

John

My skills include sleeping, laying around and incompetence.

Jim

With those set of skills you'll be exploited in no time.

Jane

Sounds like you're off to a great start.

John

I sure hope so mom.

Jim

I'm sure they'll hate you as much as we do.

John

I'll try my best.

Jane

When will you start?

John

Have you heard of any job openings?

Jim

Nope.

Jane

My job at the office is looking for part time work and my other job at the coffee shop is hiring at minimum wage. Oh and my other job…

John

But mom those jobs aren't what I want.

Jane

They're the only ones I know. Isn't there a website with jobs provided by your school?

John

Probably, but I don't go there anymore, so I don't have excess to it.

Jane

Oh, here's the newspaper.

John

Let me see it.

(John opens the newspaper and it is blank.)

Jim

There's no way of showing your incompetency now.

John

How will I be abused now?

Jim

You could change your dream to becoming a bum.

Jane

What are you going to do now?

John

What do you mean?

Jane

Your plan didn't work, so you what are you going to do?

John

I don't know.

Jim

(Moves towards John and starts showing him to the door)

Sounds like a great plan son, it's been nice seeing you. Don't bother to write. We won't read it.

John

But wait I thought I could stay here.

Jim

He's stupider than I thought.

John

But, mom there's another problem.

Jane

What?

Jim

Here come the waterworks.

John

I'm in a lot of debt from school and I have to start paying it back. I need a job right now.

Jane

Well, it looks like you're going to have to figure it out.

John

Mom, dad will you help me out with my debt until I'm on my feet?

Jim

No.

Jane

I don't know.

John

Please, mom.

Jane

I work a lot jobs just to keep this place going.

Jim

Yeah, so get out.

Jane

Not to mention I have to support your father's drinking himself to death. God knows that's a full-time job.

Jim

Yeah, and it ain't cheap either.

John

But I need help.

Jim

You should've thought of that before you came home.

Jane

How much debt could you possibly be in.

John

$100,000

Jim

That's way too much.

Jane

Well, the news says the economy is going to pick up any time now. So you'll be able to support yourself within a few months.

Jim

Yeah, and… what?

Jane

I mean I think he can stay.

Jim

Where's he going to live?

Jane

In his room.

Jim

But there's where I've been throwing my empties.

Jane

You're going to have to throw them somewhere else.

Jim

But won't you have to get another job.

Jane

I hate being here, so I won't mind.

Jim

But…but…

Jane

You'll hardly notice he's here and he can pay rent.

Jim

But he doesn't have any money.

Jane

So he'll be indebted to us.

Jim

Can we make him pay interest?

Jane

Of course.

Jim

Son, stay as long as you want.

John

Oh fine. I'll just buckle down and figure out how to get a job.

Jim

Good.

John

I hate you guys

Jim and Jane

We hate you too.

Scene II

Jim and Jane are sitting at the table. John enters.

Jane

Oh hi, John how was your day?

John

Well, I have some good news.

Jim

You're moving out.

Jane

You got a job.

John

Nope, I have a job interview.

Jane

Oh, that's good…I guess.

John

Thanks.

Jim gets up.

Jim

I'm going to drink a bottle of whiskey and pass out.

Jane

It's 10:30 a.m. already. I've got to get ready for my other job.

Jim

But before I do, I want to give you some words of wisdom, son. You're a disappointing burden to your mother and I and we regret the fact that you are our son.

John

Thanks dad.

Jim

Just doing my job.

Jim exits.

John

Mom.

Jane

Yes son.

John

I'm nervous about this interview.

Jane

Why?

John

Well, I mean when I get this job and move out and make millions of dollars, I'll forget about you and dad.

Jane

Right…

John

I'm just wondering do you think I should wear a blue tie or a red one?

Jane

Probably the red. It brings out the patheticness in your face.

John

Blue it is. Thanks.

Jane

You're welcome… oh and John.

John

Yes.

Jane

Just remember when you get the job, you'll be an adult and have to dig yourself out of your own holes.

John

Thanks mom you always know just what to say.

Jane

That's what a mother is for.

John

I love you but only because I have no money.

Jane

Oh sweetie, I love you too only because I have to.

Jane touches John's Face

Jane

Otherwise, they'd put me in prison.

Scene III

John is sitting on stage in a banana costume reading a letter. Jim is laying on the stage snoring clutching an empty bottle. Jane enters.

Jane

Hi hun, what's with the costume?

John

I got an internship with the Banana Shack down the street. I hold the sign outside of the store.

Jane

So you found a job?

John

No, it's an internship. There's no money but if I do a good job, they'll write me a strong letter of recommendation.

Jane

Well, that's a start.

John

Not the start I need. Look at this.

John hands the letter to Jane. She reads it out loud.

Jane

We are pleased to let you know we have increased the interest on your loans from one hundred percent to two hundred percent…That's a strange way to put it.

John

I just don't know what I'm going to do.

Jane

Oh honey, you'll find something. And if you don't you'll continue be indebted to your father and I.

(She checks here watch.)

I've got to get to work. See you later.

(Jane starts to leave but sees that John is really depressed.)

What's wrong?

John

There aren't any jobs out there and everything is getting worse for me.

Jane

Things are bad now but hopefully things will get better.

John

Yeah, but I need them to get better now.

Jane

Well…

(Jane walks over to where Jim is sleeping and goes through his pockets. She finds some money and hands it to John.)

John

What happened to not supporting me?

Jane

Well, I figured what's one more sacrifice.

John

Thanks, mom.

Jane

No problem honey. How about before I leave I make you a cheese sandwich?

John

Would you cut out all of the mold from the bread?

Jane

Of course, sweetie.

She quickly slaps together a sandwich and hands it to him.

John

Thanks. Will I see you later?

Jane

Maybe, after I go to work at the Taco Hut I have to work the graveyard shift at shirt factory.

John

Oh ok.

Jane

Bye.

John

Oh mom.

Jane

Yes, honey.

John

I…I hate you.

Jane

I hate you too.

Jane exits. Jim wakes up

Jim

What?

He looks around and then looks into the empty bottle.

Jim

Gotta go to the store…where's my money…damn it…did a thief come by and steal my money.

John

Thief?

Jim

The thief. Did he come by and steal my money?

John

I didn't see any thief.

Jim

Well, if you do…tell him I'm coming for him.

John

Sure will.

Jim

Why are you so bright?

John

I'm wearing a banana costume.

Jim

I thought Halloween already passed.

John

I'm have an internship at the Banana Shack.

Jim

They paying you?

John

No.

Jim

Then why are you there?

John

It might lead to a job.

Jim

Might…Lead…Jesus, how did I get a son who was so stupid?

John

Hey.

Jim

Hey yourself. They're not going to give you a job. Which mean they saw your capacity for believing in bullshit, so they put you in a yellow suit.

John

No, they said it was a great honor to don the banana suit.

Jim

I bet they did. I bet they also said we only give this to the most worthily person not everyone can pull it on.

John

Yeah so.

Jim

So, I'm saying you probably just saw a sign and thought hey I can do that.

John

Yeah.

Jim

Well, you need to stop doing that. First, you're a half-assed coward who doesn't seem to know his head's up his own ass. Secondly, no one will respect you if you just take any job. Have some self-respect.

John

But there aren't any jobs.

Jim

Are you sure or did you just give up?

John

I'm pretty sure.

Jim

Because I know how you like to give up.

John

What…no…like what have I given up on?

Jim

College.

John

I mean, ok, but what's another one.

Jim

Banana Shack.

John

I haven't given up.

Jim

You will.

John

Shut up.

Jim

See. You half-ass things. It's a family trait. Look at me, I have a job but I collect disability and workman's comp all from a little "accident" down at the box factory.

John

Really?

Jim

Yeah, been milking it for ten years.

John

So you're saying I should realize that I'm a no-good-lay-about and just accept it.

Jim

What? No. That's what you got from that? Jesus.

John

Then what did you mean?

Jim

I meant move out and never come back.

John

I'm trying.

Jim

Try hard.

John

God, I hate you.

Jim

Yeah, I hate you too.

Scene IV

Jim are sitting at the table. Jim is waiting as Jane crushes up his high blood pressure medication into his meal.

Jim

Hey, is it ready yet?

Jane

Almost.

She slides the last bit of medication into his drink and hands Jim a plate and a cup. Jim takes a giant gulp and drinks it all.

Jim

Nothing like being poisoned to start the day.

Jane

Isn't it. You want to read the newspaper.

Jim

You know I can't read.

Jane

But there are pictures.

Jim

I'll give it a look.

Jim takes a long gulp from the glass.

Jane

Boy, you drank that fast.

Jim

Well, this liver won't harden itself.

John Enters.

John

Well, I did it.

Jane

What?

John

I didn't get the job.

Jim

You're a horrible burden on your mother and I.

John

Thanks. I couldn't have done it without you.

Jane

Oh and here's your mail.

She hands some mail to Jim. He rips it open.

Jim

Oh yes, free money.

Jane

Oh John, you got some mail. It came through the window.

(Jane drops a brick on the table with a letter attached to it.)

Hit your father on the head.

John

You ok dad?

Jim

Nothing a day's worth of drinking can't fix.

John opens the letter.

Jane

What is it honey?

John

It says, "Give us our money or else. A Message from Chambers Bank, for all of your banking needs."

Jane

You didn't get a job and they're sending you threats, big day.

Jim

How are you going to celebrate?

John throws the letter down and starts walking off stage.

Jane

Where are you going?

John

My room to cry.

Jim

Nothing like a little self-hate.

Jane

When I said celebrate, I meant together.

Jane sits at the table.

Jim

If I had known I would have a coward for a son I would have tried to push you down the stairs more when you were pregnant.

Jane

You always were a romantic.

She inches closer to Jim.

Jim

No, I'm serious. I gave up my life to ignore and neglect him and this is the thanks I get. I should have run when you told me you were pregnant.

Jane

But you didn't

Jim

My car was out of gas.

Jane

Remember your hair?

Jim

Greasiest mullet in the tri-state area.

Jane

And that car.

Jim

I put a lot of miles on that Chevette.

Jane

You sure did.

She touches him.

Jim

You know this isn't going to be pretty?

Jane

I don't want it to be.

Jim

I hate you.

Jane

I hate you too.

They smoosh their faces together in a kiss and fall to the floor.

Scene V

John is sitting up in a hospital bed between Jim and Jane.

Jane

What happened?

Jim

Did you get drunk and fall down some stairs.

Jane

Oh, Jim.

Jim

What, it happened to the best of us.

John

No, I was walking out of an interview and these two well-dressed men started beating with clubs.

Jane

Oh dear.

John

They left this.

John holds up a business card. Jane takes it and reads it aloud.

Jane

For all of your banking needs. Oh, it was those debt collectors.

Jim

You must have really pissed them off.

John

They said to give them their money or else they'll break your knee caps and Thank for your cooperation Chambers Bank.

Jane

They sure do know how to advertise.

Jim

It's impressive.

John

Guys.

Jim

What it's true.

John

Can't you see I'm in pain.

Jane

Oh stop.

John

What?

Jim

You're always in pain. You know, back in my day, we used to beat the shit of each other until we straightened up and flew right. I didn't do that with you so these bankers are picking up the slack.

John

I just don't know what to do.

Jim

Give them their money.

John

But I don't have any money.

Jim

Well, I guess they're going to break your knee caps.

John

I didn't even finish school and I still own them the money.

Jim

That's how a scam works son.

John

You two said college was a good idea.

Jim

We thought it was.

John

Why would you think that?

Jim

I was probably drunk.

Jane

What I think your father is trying to say is, we thought it was a good idea because everyone else was doing it.

Jim

We thought you'd get a job and never come back and leave us alone.

Jane

Exactly.

John

It's not like I haven't been trying.

Jane

Oh, we know, but maybe try harder.

John

Well, what do you mean?

Jane

You know, try…but only harder.

John

I don't understand.

Jim

Jesus Christ, are you really that stupid. What she's saying is try harder at finding a job.

John

Yeah, but I don't know how to do that.

Jim

It's simple. Do what you're doing now only better?

John

But I'm already applying to 100 jobs a day.

Jim

Maybe try 200.

John

But you guys don't understand.

Jane

Of course, we don't honey.

Jim

Yeah, I mean I dropped out of school and got an union job, so I can never get fired.

Jane

And I've been working for so long I can get any low paying job I want.

John

How are any of those things supposed to help?

Jane

I guess they don't.

John

I need skills, but the only way to get them is to get a job and the only way to get a job is to have a skill.

Jim

I was never very good at riddles either.

Jane

I don't know the answer either John, but you'll figure it out.

John

Is that your answer? I'll figure it out.

Jane

What do you want me to say?

John

I don't know. Everything will be alright.

Jim

It wouldn't be.

Jane

I've never been in this situation.

John

But you were wrong.

Jim

Yeah, and you were gullible.

John

I have to get out of here. I have to get rid of this debt.

Jane

But how?

Jim

Fake your own death.

Jane

Or get 100% disability.

Jim

I got a baseball bat you can barrow.

John

(He stands up. And walks towards Center Downstage. Spot light on him.)
No, no none of that will work. I just hate it. Everywhere I go I think about my debt. Every time I'm out with my friends it's debt, debt, debt, when I talk to a girl, debt, when I come home alone, debt, just debt, debt, debt. It never goes away. I can't stand it.

Jim

Whoopty doo.

John

I hate you.
(Going back into the hospital bed. Lights up.)

Jim

So, do we.

Jane

Yeah, we thought you'd leave and never come back.

Jim

Now you're back miserable. It's depressing.

Jane

Makes me want to talk to your father.

Jim

See what you've done. I'm so depressed I want to go back to work.

John

Well, I'm sorry things didn't work out for you. They didn't work out for me either.

Jim

Oh boo-woo.

John

You've done nothing but cause me pain.

Jim

We didn't make you go to school.

Jane

We didn't make you take out the loan.

John

You might as well have.

Scene VI

Jim and Jane are sitting at the table reading the newspaper and John walks in.

John

Hi, mom. Hi dad.

Jim & Jane

Hi Son.

Jane

How's the job search?

John

I just got back from an interview.

Jim

Will they be exploiting you?

John

One of them to spit in my face.

Jane

That's like a good sign.

John

Hopefully.

Jane

Oh, I almost forgot you got mail.

Jane hands him a letter. John opens it.

John

Oh boy.

Jim

What is it, son?

John

It's from the debt collectors.

Jane

What did they say?

John

You're fucked.
(John show the letter to them. In big letters it says "You're Fucked.")
What does that mean?

Jim

I guess you're going to be fucked.

Jane

Seems pretty straight forward.
(Pause)
What are you going to do?

John

I'm going to kill myself.

Jim

That a boy.

John

Where are dad's high blood pressure pills.

Jane

Don't use those, I slowly killing your father with them.

John

What else is there?

Jane

The Knives are in the draw.
John gets a butter knife.

Jim

John that's a butter knife.

John

Fuck you dad.

Jim

Well, I tried.
John cuts his wrists and falls to the floor moans. Jane and Jim go on read the newspaper.

Jane

Oh look. He actually did it.

Jim

I never thought he had it in him.

Jane

I know. I'm so proud of him. He finally found a skill.

Jim

That's a lot of blood.

Jane

Should we call an ambulance?

Jim

Maybe.

Jane

He's still on our insurance.

Jim

In that case let's wait a little while.

Jim

Don't worry. The ambulance won't get here until way after he's dead.

SceneVII

Jim and Jane are sitting in a hospital waiting room.

Jane

Here's the bill.

Jim

What? I thought he was dead.

Jane

They say he's going to make it.

Jim

Can't they do something?

Jane

They've done all they can. He's going to live.

Jim

No, why me…why me?

Jane

Hey, we can get threw this.

Jim

No, don't you see. We had it all planned out. You with your working yourself to death, slowly poisoning me. And me drinking myself to death. We had it all. Now it's all gone.

Jane

Don't say that Jim. We can still have that.

Jim

No, we can't. It's gone.

Jane

I can grind up your pills. I can still kill you.

Jim

I have to confess something… I built up a tolerance.

Jane

What? No. You didn't…how could you.

Jim

Yeah, it doesn't work. All of those pills.

Jane

Why didn't you tell me?

Jim

Because I saw the joy on your face.

Jane

You bastard.

Jim

That's not important now. What's important is how to get out of this debt.

Jane

So we can go back to the way things were.

Jim

Yes. Just what I was thinking. And if you could get another job or two I think we'll make it.

Jane

Another job.

Jim

Or two.

Jane

I don't think I can.

Jim

What do you mean? Of course you can. I believe in you.

Jane

Here's an idea why don't you go back to work.

Jim

Me, but I'm trying to drink myself to death.

Jane

Well, you're going to have to put that on hold for this crisis.

Jim

No, no I'm not. I refuse. You can't make me.

Act II

Jim and John are sitting at the table. John's hands are bandaged and John is wearing a suit that is too small for him.

Jim

You want to know what I don't like about you, son?

John

Not really.

Jim

You're really inconsiderate to me and your mother.

John

What?

Jim

I mean, couldn't you have at least killed yourself. Now instead of buying a nice cheap coffin, me and your mother have to pay off all this debt. Can't you finish anything you start?

John

Apparently not.

Jim

Here I am thinking I'd spend the rest of my life drinking and being miserable but no. Turns out our insurance doesn't cover suicide attempts. So it's back to the old box factory for old Jimmy boy.

John

I thought it would have killed me.

Jim

Please John, don't lie to me. I watched you do it, you didn't even cut a main artery.

John

Sorry dad.

Jim

Don't be sorry just next time do it right. It's not across the street but down the road. Didn't they teach you that in school.

Jane enters in a daze.

Jim

Hey honey.

Jane

Would you like fries with that?

Jim

No, Jane your home.

Jane

The special today is…

(Jim gets up and shakes her.)

I was having a lovely dream I was still at work.
(Sees Jim and John)
What a nightmare it's become.
(She sits)
(Pause)
How was everyone's day?

Jim

I wish I was dead.

Jane

That good.

Jim

I tried to smash my hand into a door, but I couldn't. Now I have to go to work tomorrow.

Jane

How awful.

John

Mine was okay.

Jane

Great.

Jane

Have your cuts healed yet?

John

Almost.

Jane

Do you think you could get a job now?

Jim

Yeah, so you can help with all the financial stress you've caused us.

John

I checked the paper. I don't think there are any.

Jim

I found a job.

John

You just showed up after a ten year hiatus.

Jim

I still found it.

Jane

Oh you two.

John

I think I going to kill myself.

Jane

Are you going to finish it this time?

John

Mom. It was a…

Jim

You're mother's right. We don't have the money for you to fail again. We're just going to have to leave you here until it's finished. That could take all night.

John

But, I've tried.

Jane

I'd say try harder, but you don't listen.

Jim

Suicide and listening are not your skill set. Do you have any other skills you'd like to attempt?

John

I have skills.

Jane

Like what?

John

Well, I don't know. I can…uh… I can read a book…kind of…and I can spit pretty far.

Jane

Those might be hobbies even talents, but not skills.

John

I guess I don't have any then.

Jim

Hey, you just gave me an idea.

John

What?

Jane

Oh good.

Jim

Why don't we write resumes for John. We have skills. We have jobs. That way we can turn this incompetent mess into an incompetent mess with a job.

Jane

That just might work.

John

But what about the interview.

Jim

We'll practice.

John

But I don't believe I can do it.

Jane

You're going to have to.

Jim

Yeah, you don't have much of a choice.

John

Well, gosh. I guess so.

Jane

You know what this means?

Jim

More work.

Jane & Jim

We hate you so much.
(pause)

John

I hate you too.

Scene II

Jim and Jane are talking and writing.

Jane

How many years of experience does that job need?

Jim

1 to 2

Jane

Ok, so let's say he worked at McDonalds for three years as a cashier.

Jim

But doesn't that conflict with his job at auto mechanic.
(Pause.)

Jane

You're right.

Jim

Put he worked part time for both.

Jane

No. No. No one wants part time

Jim

Why not say two years for the mechanic and two for the cashier.

Jane

Perfect.

John enters.

John

Hey Mom, hey dad.

Jim and Jane

(Without looking up) Hey.

John

What are you guys doing?
(No answer. They continue to write and research.)

Jim

Put that he has people skills.

Jane

Oh, come on. What people skills?

Jim

I don't know. Like interpersonal skills or something like that.

Jane

Don't you think once he's in the interview will see he's a bumbling idiot.

John

I can just say I'm ner…

Jim

But the job we're applying to is working with people.

Jane

Maybe we should find another position.

Jim

No, he can just say he's nervous or something.

John

That's what I said.

Jane

Alright, but if he screws this up, we have to find another job.

John

But I can get the job.

Jim

I mean he's bound to screw it up. This is a learning process.

John

Hey.

Jane

Should we put he graduated from college.

Jim

Absolutely.

John

HEY.

Jane & Jim

WHAT.

John

Can I have a say?

Jim

No.

Jane

Fine.

John

What job are you applying me to?

Jane

A simple cashier job.

John

I don't think I'd be good at that.

Jim

Well, you're going to have to learn.

John

What? Why not?

Jane

Because you're incompetent.

John

But that's not fair.

Jim

Yeah and you messing up your suicide attempt wasn't fair either.

John

I hate you.

(Pause)

Jim

So, what should he wear?

Jane

Maybe, a blue dress shirt with a red tie.

Jim

I like the red, it symbolizes power.

They go back to work. John sits down on the ground defeated.

Scene III

John and Jane are sitting at a table. Jim passed out on the ground.

John

Is dad alright?

Jane

He's just exhausted from trying to break his bones at work.

John

Mom.

Jane

Yes.

John

Sorry I tried to kill myself.

Jane

It's alright.

John

Thanks for getting me this interview.

Jane

You're welcome.

John

You and dad were right. I couldn't have done it without you.

Jane

(She rubs his shoulder)

Glad you finally admit it.

John

I'm really nervous about this interview.

Jane

Why?

John

What if I mess up?

Jane

Do you want to practice?

John

I think so.

Jane

Ok, I'll be the interviewer.

John

Alright.
(John pretends to straighten up a tie.)
Hi, my name is…

Jane

What…oh I guess I have another interview.

John

Yes, I'm the 12 o'clock my name is…

Jane

(Pretending to pick up the phone.)
Angela, I thought I told you to tell everyone I'm out to lunch.
(Pause)

Jane

Idiot…So what were you saying?

John

I'm John…

Jane

Resume.
(John hands her the resume. She flips through it.)

Jane

I just don't think you're cut out for this line of work.

John

But you didn't even look at my resume.

Jane

Don't need to. I just know.

John

Can't be that hard to be a cashier.

Jane

Are you giving me lip?

John

No mam.

Jane

That's what I thought. Just because you got some college you think your better than me.

John

No…I never…

Jane

Get out.

(Silence.)

Jane

How was that?

John

What I excepted.

Jane

So what's there to worry about?

John

I guess I was just being stupid.

Jane

Well, John that's why we wrote the resume for you.

Scene IV

John is sitting alone at the table in a suit and tie depressed. Jane enters.

Jane

How'd the interview go?

John

It went great.

Jane

Really.

John

Yeah, I got the job.

Jane

You finally have someone to exploit you.

John

Just what I wanted.

Jane

Then what's wrong?

John

I saw woman handing out pamphlets on debt.

Jane

What did the pamphlets say?

John

I don't know.

Jane

Didn't you get one?

John

She gave me one once I told her I had debt, but took it away when I said it defaulted.

Jane

You weren't her audience.

John

She looked at me like I was a leper.

Jane

Look, now that you have this job you'll be able to pay us back and pay off some of your debt.

John

Yeah, but I won't be able to have fun.

Jane

Well, that's what you get.

John

For what being scammed.

Jane

Precisely.

John

But I didn't know I got scammed until it was too late.

Jane

Well, at least now you know.

Jim enters angry.

Jim

I tell you I just can't win.

Jane

Why do you say that?

Jim

I try to step into front of a fork lift, they stop it. I try to lay down on the convey-er belt, they take me off. I tell you it's like no one wants me to get workmen's comp.

Jane

Have you tried slipping on something in the bathroom? You know where there aren't any cameras.

Jim

Yes, but they put an assistant in there at all times now.

Jane

Sounds fancy.

Jim

It's pretty nice, but apparently three other workers have slipped and sued.

Jane

Sounds like they beat you to the punch.

Jim

I'm the manager. I should slip first. There's a hierarchy.
(Pause)
Anyway, how was everyone else's day.

John

I got a job.

Jane

Well, at my first job, I saw this lady wearing…

Jim

Wait, shut up for a second…
(Jane stops talking).
What did you say?

John

I got a job.

Jim

Well, you finally found someone to exploit you.

John

Yeah, and it's a pretty easy…
(Jim waves his hand in disgust.)

Jim

I don't care about that. How much do you get paid?

John

Minimum wage.

Jim

Minimum wage. (Jim starts to think.) Great. You see I have great ideas.

Jane

Yeah, we get it. You're great.

Jim

Jealous.

Jane

I really don't re…

Jim

You just wanted to let him figure it out... Idiot.

Jane

Alright. I already said you…

Jim

As if that's ever worked.

Jane

I wish I could poison you still.

Jim

That ship has sailed.

Scene V

Jim, Jane, and John are all at the table.

Jane

How was everyone's day.

Jim and John

I wish I was dead.

Jane

So what else is new.

Jim

Let me tell you it's not easy being incompetent. I have to remember not to wear googles or not to mop the floors or even to fix shelves so they won't fall.

John

Sounds tough.

Jim

It is. Why just today, a box exploded right next to me, but because of my goggles I was ok.

Jane

Wow and to think if it had you could have gone back on disability.

Jim

Yeah, and you know what I was think?

John

No, what?

Jim

That's the problem I wasn't thinking.

Jane

I know what that's like. I fell asleep at the fry-o-lator and my managers hair caught fire. As she was running around screaming. I thought I wish that were me.

Jim

Damn. It could've been.

Jane

What about you John, how's your work?

John

Well, I come in and the manager chains me to the wall and screams at me to write blog posts.

Jane

Wow, that's so inspiring.

Jim

Now that's a good manager.

Jane

I wish my managers cared that much about me.

John

I mean I really don't like it. I don't really write I just copy other blog posts say their mine.

Jim

Let me tell you something no one likes work.

John

Sure, but you'd think there'd be something productive being done.

Jim

Why?

John

Well, because they're hard to get.

Jane

Oh John, you have so much to learn.

Jim

Yeah, work isn't about being productive. It's about being paid to be abused.

Jane

I get whipped daily at all of my jobs.

Jim

Sometimes I tie one of my workers up and beat him just to show they still have a purpose.

John

That sounds terrible.

Jane

Isn't this what you wanted to be exploited?

John

Yeah, but I thought I'd at least find happiness. Not get beat.

Jane and Jim laugh.

Jane

Oh John, you're so naive.

Jim

Yeah, this is the real world. There is no happiness.

Scene VI

John is holding an envelope with Jim and Jane over his shoulder.

Jane

Come on John don't keep us waiting see how much you made this week.

John

Can't you just calculate that?

Jim

Where's the fun in that.

John opens the envelop. Takes out pay stub.

John

I made…

Suddenly, Jim and Jane both jump at the check, but Jim gets it first.

Jane

Hey, I deserve some of that.

Jim

You'll have to fight me for it.

Jane

Fine.

She jumps at him. They begin to fight. Rolling on the floor.

Jane

It's mine.

Jim

Fuck you.

Jane

I deserve it more.

Jim

Let go.

Jim and Jane both have a hand on it and start to read.

Jane

You made…

Jim

zero dollars.

Jane

How is that possible?

Jim

Right here, taxes and debt 100%

Jane

100%.

John

So you're saying I make no money.

Jim

Big fat goose egg.

John

But how am I going to pay you back or pay off my debt?

Jim

Get another job.

Jane

Oh you could work under the table.

Jim

Yeah, maybe you could learn to hustle.

Jane

Are you good at manipulating people?

John

I don't think so.

Jim

Of course, he's not. Look at him he barely got this job.

John

I mean what's the point in going to work tomorrow?

Jim

Suffering.

Jane

Making your manager feel better about themselves.

John

So I'm only living to pay back my debt.

Jane

Sounds about right.

John

So then I was told a bunch of bullshit about college just so I could go into debt.

Jim

Yeah, you really ate it up too.

John

My whole life is debt.

Jim

Don't fell so bad my whole life was about making you.

Jane

Sweetie look at the positive.

John

What's the positive?

Jane

You'll never be alone.

John

What?

Jane

Wherever you go whatever you do your debt will be there. Watching you. Judging you.

Jim

It's like you got married only you go into it wishing you were dead.

John

How am I supposed to better myself?

Jane

You don't.

Jim

That was a lie anyway.

Jane

Yeah, you were always useless.

Jim

We just hoped we'd never see you again.

Jane

And how do you think we feel about all of this?

Jim

We were planning on slowly killing each other until one of us was alone. Now we can't even do that.

Jane

We have to take care of you forever.

Jane and Jim throw the check at John's feet and walk off stage.

John

I hate you.

Scene VII

Jim and Jane are sitting at the table with a pile of money. They are drinking champagne and laughing. Jim has a bandage on his head.

Jane

We did it.

Jim

We sure did. No more bills.

Jane

I can't believe you got 100%

Jim

I can't either for a crack on the head.

Jane

You sure fooled them.

Jim

It wasn't even that hard.

Jane

Maybe I should too.

Jim

Yeah, because this is all mine.

Jane

Not any of it.

Jim

Nope.

Jim keeps drinking and Jane stares angrily. John enters holding a bag.

John

Hey

Jim

Hey, what's going on?

John

Where'd all this money come from?

Jane

Your father slipped and cracked his head at work.

Jim

100% disability. Woo.

Jane

We paid off the hospital debt.

Jim

And we still have money.

Jane

But how was work?

John

I quit.

Jane

What?

Jim

Why'd you do that?

John

Because there was no point in having one.

Jane

But who'll exploit you now?

John

I'm not sure I want that anymore.

Jane

Oh John don't give up on your dreams.

Jim

Going somewhere.

John

Oh yeah. I'm moving out.

Jim

Finally.

Jane

What? Where?

John

I found someone with a couch in the city, so I decided to go there.

Jane

Are there jobs in the city?

John

I don't know.

Jane

How are you going to pay rent?

John

I don't know.

Jane

But why move out you have a bed and food here.

John

I've been thinking and I really don't like you two.

Jim

For the record we don't like you either.

John

So to escape all of the negativity and guilt I decided this was a better option.

Jane

But you'll be more poor then here.

John

Yeah, but I'll be guilt free.

Jane

Guilt? What?

John

I feel guilty I put you into debt…

Jim

As you should.

John

…and I feel guilty that I couldn't live up to your expectations…

Jim

They really weren't that high.

John

…and I feel guilty I couldn't pay my debts.

Jim

Imagine how the bank felt putting you in the hospital.

John

I just felt awful. Then I thought sure this is my fault. I can't change that. But I can change my surroundings and maybe that'll be better. Even if it makes me poor.

Jim

That's stupid.

John

Why?

Jim

I'd rather feel guilt than be poor.

John

Why?

Jim

Because when you're guilty you can still make money. When you're poor you'll never be satisfied. You're suffering without any benefit.

John

I can't stand guilt. Looking at myself in the mirror knowing I'm helpless. That this is life and it will go on eternally.

Jim

I'd rather play it safe.

John

Well, I'm taking a risk.

Jim

Risk is stupid.

John

So be it.

Jane

You know I'd think you'd be happy to see John leave.

Jim

I am, but he's stupid. He'll just going to fail and end up back here.

John

Yeah, I think you're stupid.

Jim

Good for you.

John

You have to crack your head just to make a living, that's stupid.

Jim

Better than being poor.

John

No, it isn't because you'll never be satisfied. You'll always have to make sure you're awful enough to get the money. I can't live like that.

Jim

I think I've heard enough.

Jane

Jim stop. John don't leave.

John

Mom…dad…goodbye.

John exits.

Jim

First, I crack my head and my son moved out. Everything we always wanted.

Jane.

Yeah, everything we wanted.

Jim

Oh, cheer up. I'm sure I'll be dead soon and all of this will be yours.

Jane

Even the car with the rust on it.

Jim

Yes, even that.
Jane starts to cry.

Jim

Tears of joy.
(Pause)
Because of the car isn't.

Jane

No.

Jim

Then what's wrong?

Jane

Who am I going to hate now?

Jim

You can always hate me.

Jane

You're no fun to hate.

Jim

But I'm the best you got.

Jane

You don't get offended and you're passed out all the time.

Jim

That sounds like things to hate.

Jane

I guess so.

Jim

You can still poison me.

Jane

I thought you said you built up a tolerance.

Jim

Well, I mean there are lots of poisons out there.

Jane

You mean it?

Jim

Would I lie?

Jane

You mean I could kill you slowly again?

Jim

Or fast. Whatever your heart desires.

Jane

Ok, then

Jim

Come now. Dry your tears. We have our who lives ahead of us.
(A timer dings.)

Jim

What was that?

Jane

I was so happy I baked a cake.

Jim

How could this day get any better?
Jane goes off stage and comes back with a cake.

Jane

Here you go.

Jim

Looks awful.

Jane

I followed the directions.

Jim

Smells awful too.

Jane

Well, I added a few more ingredients.

Jim

I'll get a knife.
Jim gets up to get a knife and Jane starts to take money from the pile and put it in her pocket. Jim comes back with the knife in hand and sees what's going on.

Jim

You.

Jane

What?

Jim

You're the thief.

Jane

Whatever do you mean?

Jim takes the knife and cuts her throat. Jane hits her head on the table dead. Jim goes and sits down.

Jim

Alone at last.

He cuts a piece of cake and starts to eat.

Jim

Awful…what's in…this cake…oh no…Poison…

He starts choking and dies.

Curtain.

A General Dilemma

Characters

General- Narrator of the play.

Lieutenant- Leader of the remaining army. Trying to ready the soldiers for an offensive.

McCarthy- Optimist. Soldier who wants to leave to help his family.

Brown- Suicidal Volunteer who wants to continue being involved in the army.

Rodriguez- Soldier who begins to realize they might be free from the army.

Man #1- Soldier in the People's Army.

Man #2- Soldier in the People's Army.

Setting

On the front lines of a forever war. The soldiers are in a bunker made of sand-bags and a door in the center.

There is an American flag with a Dollar sign where the stars should be. The flag is well lit though the stage is dark. The sound of military drums. A general with many medals walks out on stage.

General

Ladies and Gentlemen, tonight I bring you a tale from the front lines. Our soldiers, outnumbered and outgunned, but not giving up on our liberty and laws. Continuing to fly the flag of freedom in the face of our tyrannous enemy. An enemy which wants to dismantle our values and stomp out dignity. Our soldiers are here to stop them in their tracks. Tonight, on the eve of the final push to defeat the enemy once and for all. Watch our citizens overcome and prevail for you and for me. Enjoy.

Lights up. The back of the stage is a wall made of sandbags with a door in the middle. Bones are scattered all over the place. A blackboard with a map pinned to it. Three men stand at attention while a Lieutenant points at the map.

Lieutenant

And tomorrow we'll attack here and here. Johnson will lead the first unit and assault…

(McCarthy rises his hand)

Yes, private.

McCarthy

Johnson's dead.

Lieutenant

Alright.

(Looking around at the three men)

McCarthy you'll lead the charge.

McCarthy

By myself?

Lieutenant

Well… (Looks around again) yes. We only have one bullet. So, make it count. Rodriguez you'll lead the charge directly into enemy lines.

Rodriguez

Yes, sir.

Lieutenant

Expect heavy causalities. I will give covering fire.

Rodriguez

But we only have one bullet.

Lieutenant

I'll distract the enemy by shouting insults.

Rodriguez

Those must be some insults.

Lieutenant

Let's hope so, for your sake. Now any questions about tomorrow's assault?

(Brown rises his hand)

Yes. Private Brown.

Brown

I don't have anything to do.

Lieutenant

You'll clean up the barracks and sort the mail.

Brown

But that's boring.

Lieutenant

Well, we can't trust you with a gun.

Brown

Since when.

Lieutenant

Since you tried to kill yourself.

Brown

But I just wanted some attention.

Lieutenant

Well, you got it. Cleaning duty until further notice.

Brown

But…

Rodriguez

No one's giving you a gun.

Brown

Fine.
(crosses his arms. Pouting.)

Lieutenant

Alright, let's get to the mail.
(Brown throws the mail out of his pockets. The Lieutenant picks it up as he drops it.)
Joel

McCarthy

Dead.

Lieutenant

O'Connor

McCarthy

Dead.

Lieutenant

McCarthy you have mail.

McCarthy

Cool.
(He opens it. He focuses on it really hard.)

Lieutenant

Maynard.

Brown

Here.

Lieutenant

Where?

Brown

Here.
(Brown picks up the skull. Speaking in an English accent.)
Hello, Hello, hello.

Rodriguez

Jesus Christ.

Brown

Did I get a letta from me mum?

Lieutenant

Stop it god damn it.
(Brown puts down the skull)
For the love of God bury these bones.

Brown

But I'm not on burial duty.

Lieutenant

Now you are.

Brown

But it's a conflict of interest.

Lieutenant

How?

Brown

I happen to believe the bones bring the room together.

Lieutenant

It's an order.

Brown

Fine
(Picks up a broom. Sweeps in a general direction.)

Rodriguez

Anything for me?

Lieutenant

No, sorry. Not today.

Rodriguez

It's alright.

Lieutenant

But we have all this propaganda.

Rodriguez

Sure.
Lieutenant hands Rodriguez a stack of papers.

Scene II
Rodriguez has a drum. Brown has a flag. McCarthy playing flute.

Lieutenant

And a 1 and a 2…
(Flute out of tone and the drum is off.)

Brown

Jose can't you see that Don's not really alright. what's so proudly hand fills was so gallantly stream…

Lieutenant

Those aren't the words and you're all out of time.

Rodriguez

We put a little razzle-dazzle on it.

McCarthy

What did you expect? We're not accomplished musicians.

Rodriguez

Yeah, why are we doing this?

Lieutenant

Tradition.

Brown

Can we come up with a new tradition?

Lieutenant

What's wrong with all of you? Don't you love your country?

McCarthy

It's alright.

Lieutenant

Cowards.

Rodriguez

How do you think we're still alive.

Lieutenant

Ok, let's take a break and come back in ten minutes.
(Brown grabs a broom. Lieutenant organizes some papers. McCarthy goes and sits. Pulls out the letter. Rodriguez goes over to McCarthy.)

Rodriguez

Love Letter?

McCarthy

What?

Rodriguez

You've been reading that letter since you got it.

McCarthy

It's from my mother

Rodriguez

Anything good.

McCarthy

My father and brother were accidentally killed when a plane dropped napalm on them.

Rodriguez

Yikes.

McCarthy

Now my mother is going to lose the farm.

Rodriguez

Let's hope this war ends so you can get home.

McCarthy

I'm not sure my heart's in it anymore.

Rodriguez

Oh are you in contract negotiations?

McCarthy

What? No, I volunteered.

Rodriguez

Really?

McCarthy

Yeah, how'd you get here?

Rodriguez

Thought I signed up for an internship. Then I was walking down the street a van full of men came and put a bag over my head. Next thing I knew I was in basic training.

McCarthy

Jez.

Rodriguez

Yeah, turns out I signed a life contract for the army.

McCarthy

What does your family think?

Rodriguez

Don't know. I don't think they wanted me around.

McCarthy

Sorry.

Rodriguez

This is better anyway.
(Pause)
But you volunteered?

McCarthy

Yup. I believed in all that propaganda. For Freedom and Liberty…

Rodriguez and McCarthy

For all people
(They both laugh.)

Rodriguez

Do you still believe?

McCarthy

Nope.

Rodriguez

At all.

McCarthy

No, but you do?

Rodriguez

I go back and forth.

McCarthy

I believe in that army of liberation more than I believe in anything the army tells me.

Rodriguez

You believe that?

McCarthy

Don't you?

Rodriguez

I mean I like the idea that AWOL soldiers from both sides created a liberating army in no man's land. It's a little hard to believe.

McCarthy

But where do they go?

Brown

Dead.

McCarthy

You don't know that.

Brown

I've been out there. Didn't see any liberation army. The only bones.

Rodriguez

Well, I guess that settles it.

McCarthy

Nothing is settled.
(McCarthy whispers to Rodriguez)
What if they existed. We could hook up with them. Free ourselves. Free the enemy. Not fight this battle. We could all just go home.

Rodriguez

You could save your mother's farm.

McCarthy

Yeah. What would you do?

Rodriguez

I don't know.

McCarthy

If the army exists you could do whatever you wanted.

Rodriguez

That's a big if. I'll take my chances with the dying tomorrow.

McCarthy

Well, I'm not dying here.

(McCarthy gets up and walks towards the lieutenant)

Rodriguez

Wait…what?

McCarthy

Lieutenant, I want to request leave.

Lieutenant

You know all leave is suspended until further notice.

McCarthy

But I have to go home.

Lieutenant

Nothing I can do.

McCarthy

But…

Lieutenant

We all want to go home but we have a duty here.

McCarthy

But my mother…

Lieutenant

We all have mothers and fathers and farms and jobs that need us. But if we don't fight there will be nothing to fight for.

McCarthy

To hell with this.

(McCarthy starts walking towards the door.)

Lieutenant

If you walk out that door it's treason.

(McCarthy opens the door.)

If your mother isn't dead now, she will be. Everyone will be. And this temper tantrum will have been in vain.

(McCarthy hesitates. Slams the door. Sits down. The Lieutenant walks over to him.)

Now get some rest because tomorrow is a big day.

Scene III

Lights down. Everyone's asleep on the floor. McCarthy stands up. Looks around. Silently walks towards the door. Brown sits up. They look at each other. Brown shakes his head. McCarthy walks out.

Scene IV

McCarthy is tied up. Rodriguez and Brown and the Lieutenant all have guns. Lieutenant reads from a paper.

Lieutenant

By the power vested by the Empire of these Federalist States I here by condemn Private McCarthy to be shot by firing squad for the act of desertion and treason.

Rodriguez

Why do we all have guns? We only have one bullet.

Lieutenant

So, no one knows who shot the fatal blow.

McCarthy

You don't have to do this.

(They all point their guns at McCarthy)

We don't have to fight. We can all go home.

Lieutenant

On my mark.

(He rises his free hand. Everyone points their guns at McCarthy.)

Fire.

(He drops his hand. Brown puts the gun to his head. Pulls the trigger repeatedly. Clicking. Empty. Lieutenant clicks empty. Rodriguez didn't fire.)

Rodriguez

Empty good.

(He points the gun at the Lieutenant. Shoots him dead.)

Brown

What did you do that for?

Rodriguez

Because we're cowards.

(Goes and unties McCarthy.)

McCarthy

Thanks.

Brown

What are we going to do now?

Rodriguez

I don't know. (To McCarthy) what do you think?

Lights go down.

Act II

Military drums off beat. The General comes out hurried and disheveled.

The General

Have no fear this mutiny will be crushed by the true heroes coming to bring these traitors to…

Rodriguez

(Off stage. From behind the General)
Hey, shut up.
(The General looks behind him flustered.)

The General

(Yelling behind him)
I am your superior…
(A skull is thrown from the black.)

McCarthy

Who cares.
(He starts walking off stage.)

The General

You don't scare me. I was in the battle of…

Rodriguez

Shut up or we'll beat you to death.

The General

I'll show you.
(General is off stage. Lights up. Rodriguez and McCarthy are arguing. While Brown is sweeping)

Rodriguez

What do you mean you don't know?

McCarthy

Why would you think I knew anything about leading?

Rodriguez

Because you talk about the people's liberation army.

McCarthy

Army of Liberation and it was just talk. It doesn't exist.

Rodriguez

If it doesn't exist, we can make it exist.

McCarthy

I just want to go home.

Rodriguez

Brown, can you believe this guy?
(Brown continues to swipe)
Brown, what are you doing?

Brown

My job.

Rodriguez

Why? we're free.

Brown

I like this better.

McCarthy

Didn't you want to kill yourself?

Brown

No bullets.

Rodriguez

I can offer you some rope.

Brown

There's still the plan.

Rodriguez

The lieutenant's dead. There's no plan anymore.

Brown

Does the enemy know that?

Rodriguez

We'll just barricade ourselves in here until it's over.

McCarthy

You can. I'm leaving

Rodriguez

You can't leave.

McCarthy

Watch me.

Rodriguez

But we're supposed to build a true people's liberation army.

McCarthy

Good luck with that.

(Started walking towards the door. Rodriguez grabs him. They push and shove each other.)

We don't even have bullets.

Rodriguez

We can still fight.

McCarthy

With what, love.

Rodriguez

It's a start.

(A whistle and bomb exploding. Dirt starts falling from the ceiling. Brown goes and swipes it up.)

McCarthy

Shit.

Rodriguez

No way out now.

McCarthy
Maybe…
Rodriguez
You'll be shot by both sides.
McCarthy
Only if I'm caught.
Rodriguez
You've already been caught
McCarthy
Now you're rubbing that in my face.
Rodriguez
We can build a people's liberation army.
McCarthy
We'll die.
Rodriguez
We're going to die anyway.
(McCarthy thinks about it.)
McCarthy
You're right.
(He moves away from the door)
So what were you thinking?
Rodriguez
No ranks.
McCarthy
So far I like it.
Rodriguez
Shoot the generals on all sides.
McCarthy
Already started that.
Rodriguez
Democratic vote. All of us have to agree.
McCarthy
Consensus. I'm for that. All in favor say Aye.
Rodriguez
Aye.
Brown
Nope.
McCarthy
There goes that idea.
Rodriguez
Say yes.
Brown
Alright yes.

Rodriguez

100% consensus.

Brown

Can I have a gun?

McCarthy

Absolutely not.

Brown

Can I change my vote?

Rodriguez

No, moving on.

McCarthy

Don't worry just be a cog in the wheel.

Brown

Alright.

Rodriguez

We should probably work on our recruitment.

McCarthy

Maybe we should write a manifesto.

Rodriguez

I don't have anything else to do.

Scene 2

The stage is dark with a light still on the flag. Brown, McCarthy, and Rodriguez go and lower the flag. Once lowered McCarthy takes out scissors and cut out the emblem out of the flag and hoist it back in its place. They turn to the audience.

All

Oh say can't you see
That we are completely free
For the rabble has finally won
Oh wasn't it fun
Everyone's singing in liberation
At the dissolving of every nation
From the bodies neatly stacked
To the fields of bullet riddled shacks
A new die has been casted
By the sound of a shotgun blast
Lights out.

Scene 3

Bombs are going off. McCarthy is at a typewriter typing franticly. Brown is swiping. Rodriguez is holding the door closed. He falls from an explosion and the door swings open and a grenade rolls in. Rodriguez picks it up and throws it out the door. Slams the door.

Rodriguez

How's the manifesto going?

McCarthy

(Clears throat)

We are the People's Liberation Army. Would you like to Join? Check Yes or No.

Brown

A real bard of the people.

(The door open swings open and a grenade rolls in and Rodriguez causally kicks it out)

Rodriguez

It's great.

(Rodriguez takes the note and puts it in an envelope. Walks towards the door.)

Propaganda bomb.

(Throws it out the door.)

Brown

You showed them.

Rodriguez

What do we do now?

McCarthy

I guess now we wait.

Rodriguez

Oh, for the liberation to happen.

Brown

Weren't we already liberated?

Rodriguez

I meant them. The others. To shoot their generals.

McCarthy

Yeah, whenever they find the letter.

Rodriguez

Oh yeah. The letter.

McCarthy

What is it?

Rodriguez

It didn't go very far.

McCarthy

Go out and get it then.

Rodriguez

(Pause)

Naw, let's just wait.

McCarthy

You don't want to go and get it do you?

Rodriguez

No.

(Brown stops sweeping)

Brown

I'll go and get it.

Rodriguez

No, just leave it alone.

Brown

It's fine. I'll just go and get it.

Rodriguez

I said no.

Brown

What are you going to do about?

McCarthy

Everybody calm down.
(Brown starts towards the door.)

Rodriguez

I'll beat you up.

Brown

With what? All your precious freedom.

Rodriguez

Don't you talk about freedom like that.
(Rodriguez runs towards Brown and starts strangling them. McCarthy tries to break it up.)

Brown

(choking)
So this is freedom.
(The bombing stops.)

McCarthy

Hey, the bombing stopped.
(Rodriguez doesn't stop strangling Brown)

Rodriguez

But why?

Brown

Maybe they decided war wasn't for them and went home.
(Rodriguez lets go of Brown)

Rodrigucz

Don't be stupid. They found our letter.

Brown

Yeah, I'm sure that's it.
(A knock at the door.)

McCarthy

Did anyone else hear that?

Brown

The knock

McCarthy

Yeah.

Brown

Who could that be?

Rodriguez

Maybe it's the people's liberation army.

(Rodriguez runs to the doors and McCarthy holds it closed.)

McCarthy

What if it isn't?

Brown

I guess you're fucked.

Rodriguez

We're fucked.

Brown

Says you. I'm going to make myself useful and show my sweeping skills.

McCarthy

Good luck with that.

Rodriguez

Who is it?

Act III

Lights up on the General standing in the middle of the stage. He spews blood and falls down with a knife in his back. Lights up.

Voice

Open the door.

McCarthy

Not until you tell us who it is.

Voice

Your mother.

McCarthy

(Opening the door.)
My mother.

Two men in army fatigues and guns come into the room.

Man #1

What's up?

McCarthy

Nothing?

Man #2

Who are you?

Rodriguez

We'd ask you the same question.

Man #1

Well, we got the guns so you go first.

Rodriguez

We're the 6th… no 7th infinitary…

McCarthy

7th ½ infinitary.

Rodriguez

Yeah, that's it. I think.

Man #1

Not anymore. From here on out you are a part of the people's army.
(Rodriguez lights up.)

Rodriguez

The People's Liberation Army. It actually exists.

Man #1

Whoa. We're the People's Army. No liberation.

McCarthy

So, you're AWOL soldiers trying to set humanity free.

Man #2

No, we're made up of soldiers who got bored fighting other people's wars, so we decide to fight our own.

Man #1

And we shoot deserters.

Rodriguez

How'd you guys come to start your own army?

Man #1

We found a letter to join a people's army or whatever. We checked yes. Then shot the generals

McCarthy

Told you it'd work.

Brown

They seem like real stand up guys.

Rodriguez

And everyone joined you?

Man #2

Sure, if they don't, we shoot them and burned their bodies.

McCarthy and Rodriguez

Oh.

McCarthy

Where do we sign up?

Brown

Hold on. So all we get is to survive if we join?

Man #1

You'll get food and shelter and…

Brown

Do we get guns?

Man #1

Of course.

Brown

Can I have one right now?

Man #2

Sure.

(the Man #2 handed Brown a Gun)

McCarthy

Actually, we don't give…

(Brown puts the gun in his mouth and pulls the trigger. Falls to the floor dead.)

Never mind.

Rodriguez

Holy shit.

Man #1

Well, one less mouth to feed.

Man #1

Here are some brochures for new recruits.

(Man #2 hands them some brochures. McCarthy and Rodriguez flip through the brochure. Rodriguez raises his hand.)

Man #1

What.

Rodriguez

There are ranks in this army?

Man #1

Of course.

Man #2

What else would we have?

Rodriguez

I don't know like revolutionary militias organized by love.

Man #1

PFFFT.
(Makes the Jerk Off motion.)
Get a load of this guy.

Man #2

What does that even mean?

Rodriguez

It means liberating people against oppression.

Man #1

No, we'd prefer raping and pillaging.

Man #2

Yeah, our program is on the back.

Rodriguez

Well, don't we get to vote.

Man#2

No.

Rodriguez

How is this any different from any other army?

Man #1

We run it.

Rodriguez

Why would anyone want to join your army?

Man #2

Because we'll kill you if you don't join.

Rodriguez

Oh.
(McCarthy finishes the brochure and approaches the men.)

McCarthy

Well, seems like everything's in order we're ready to join.

Man #1

Great. Carry our back packs.

Rodriguez

No.

Man #2

That was an order.

Rodriguez

I don't want to join.

Man #1

We have another brochure for people who can't read.

McCarthy

Hey, man. This is our chance to be a part of a real army of the people.

Rodriguez

This isn't it.

McCarthy

Close enough.

Rodriguez

They want to rape and pillage.

McCarthy

That could lead to liberation.

Rodriguez

Are you serious?

McCarthy

We came all this way, now you're just going to throw it away.

Rodriguez

You're throwing it away by taking sides with these goons.

Man #1

Hey, we can here you.

(Rodriguez walks up to the two men.)

Rodriguez

Shoot me.

McCarthy

No, don't think this is the way. Please.

Rodriguez

I've already made my decision.

(Man #1 and Man #2 look at each other and shrug.)

Man #1

You want this one.

Man #2

If you don't want to.

Man #1

Naw you can. I'm kind of sore.

(Man #2 takes out his gun. McCarthy stands in front of Rodriguez.)

McCarthy

He's just joking. It's been a long day.

Rodriguez

Get out of the way.

McCarthy

Come on. Stop already.

Man #2

He looks serious.

Man #1

Yeah, move. We got some raping and pillaging to do.

Rodriguez

This is what I want.

McCarthy

Fine.

(McCarthy move away. Man #2 shoots Rodriguez.)

Man #1

Shame. Would've made a fine private.

Man #2

Makes a good corpse though.

(The two men start walking off stage. McCarthy looks at Rodriguez's corpse.)

Man #1

You and your jokes.

Man #2

Did you hear the one about your mother?

Man #1

No, what about her?

Man #2

She's fat.

(Man #1 laughs. He looks back at McCarthy)

Man #1

You coming or what?

Man #2

Don't forget our back packs.

(The two men walk off stage. McCarthy grabs the back packs and starts walking off stage. Looks back one last time. Exits.)

Scene II

The stage is dark. McCarthy, Man #1 and Man #2 come on stage. They lower the American flag and put a new symbol of a fist in the hole. They hoist it back up to its original position. All three sing.

All

Oh, say, can you see? By the dawn's early light
What so proudly we hailed at the twilight's last gleaming;
Whose broad stripes and bright stars, through the perilous fight,
O'er the ramparts we watched were so gallantly streaming.
And the rocket's red glare, the bombs bursting in air.
Gave proof through the night that our flag was still there:
Oh, say, does that star-spangled banner yet wave?
O'er the land of the free and the home of the brave!

Lights down.